M000248171

DIVIDED DESTINY

A History of Japanese Americans in Seattle

BY DAVID A. TAKAMI

University of Washington Press, Seattle & London
Wing Luke Asian Museum, Seattle

Cover photo: The Sugino family in 1928, from left: Frank (age 7), Tizo (41), Michiko (4), Mikio (9), Nobuko (2), Mitsuya (33), and Sally (8). Courtesy Seattle Buddhist Temple Archives, Henry and Yuki Miyake Collection.

Book designed by Paula Onodera Wong

This book was originally published as a booklet accompanying the 1992 exhibition *Executive Order 9066: 50 Years Before and 50 Years After,* at the Wing Luke Asian Museum.

Publication was supported by the Civil Liberties Public Education Fund.

Copyright © 1998 by the Wing Luke Asian Museum
Printed in the United States of America

Wing Luke Asian Museum
407 Seventh Avenue South
Seattle, Washington 98104

All rights reserved. No part of this publication may be reproduced or transmitted in any form or by any means, electronic or mechanical, including photocopy, recording, or any information storage or retrieval system, without permission in writing from the publisher.

ISBN 0-295-97762-0
Library of Congress Catalog Card Number: 98-61175

The paper used in this publication meets the minimum requirements of American National Information Sciences—Permanence of Paper for Printed Library Materials, ANSI Z39.48-1984.

TABLE OF CONTENTS

FOREWORD

SHORTLY AFTER I WAS HIRED as the new director of the Wing Luke Asian Museum in February 1991, I initiated an experimental exhibit project that would become the model in spirit for every exhibit to follow.

This display, *Executive Order 9066: 50 Years Before and 50 Years After,* opened on February 19, 1992, the 50-year anniversary of the infamous federal order that forced 110,000 Japanese Americans to forsake their homes for desolate concentration camps.

The specific focus of the exhibit was to tell, in the voices of the former camp inmates and their children, the painful story of the wartime injustice: the loss of property, rights, and precious freedom; the struggles to resist the incarceration and survive camp conditions; the diligent efforts to rebuild lives and heal profound emotional wounds; and the attempts, finally, to seek justice from a government that had coldly breached their trust.

"You can't create a quality exhibit," I was duly warned in the beginning, "if you put the work in the hands of a committee. You'll have too much infighting, too many egos, no artistic control."

I wasn't convinced. The "9066" experiment—grounded on the premise that a museum should be a living laboratory for the collaborative talents of ordinary people, not simply a place for a small group of specialists—defied the fears of the skeptics. The exhibit drew over 50,000 visitors to our small facility over a seven-month run. It was more successful than any exhibit ever assembled by the museum in its 25-year history and brought national acclaim to a once-quiet neighborhood cultural institution.

During the course of a year, over 100 individuals from the local Japanese American community came to the museum to work on the project, forging deep relationships among themselves as they learned, planned, shared, gathered information, conducted interviews, designed, wrote, and built the exhibit. They met across the vast generation gulf, leaving behind old grudges and political differences, to bring this endeavor to life. The display was stellar in every respect, garnering, as proof, several awards, many outstanding reviews, and the respect of the museum community.

The exhibit moved me emotionally in a way few other exhibits have, before or since. I recall walking down to the exhibit floor and hearing, from behind display walls, the animated chatter of the second-generation Nisei discovering familiar faces: "Holy smokes! Why that's—" From there, the retelling of countless stories would begin. I would see visitors emerge from the replica of a barrack from Minidoka—constructed in painstaking detail by Bob Shimabukuro—to talk about their sense of betrayal by the government, revealing deep anguish at seeing parents "broken" during the years of incarceration. In the alcove display on the Nisei veterans, I would see family members, huddled in reflective silence, sobbing, remembering the loss of brothers and uncles who had sacrificed their lives in hopes of banishing public doubts about Japanese American loyalty to this country.

The success of the "Executive Order 9066" experiment set the stage for the Wing Luke Asian Museum to reimagine itself as a vehicle for community organizing and empowerment, and to carry out similar landmark historical exhibits on Chinese Americans, Vietnamese Americans, and other groups. In a mighty way, the "Executive Order 9066" exhibit affirmed the restorative power of the oral tradition and the first-person voice of ordinary people. It gave sanction, in a museum setting, to the notion of students, nonprofessionals, and elders as researchers and lead decision makers, rather than token advisors.

In the years since "Executive Order 9066" came down, a smaller traveling version of the original exhibit has continued to visit libraries, schools, and community centers. Still, there have been numerous calls for a permanent installation that brings back into public view the central pieces of the display. That dream will be realized in the near future when the museum undertakes a capital campaign to develop an expanded facility, with more room for displays.

The museum has received many requests for a reprint of the "Executive Order 9066" exhibit catalog. This attractive booklet featured an original narrative history of Japanese Americans in Seattle by David Takami and reproductions of photos from the exhibit. David, a freelance journalist, also served as oral historian, exhibit-text writer, and all-purpose editor for the "9066" project. David—in his patient, efficient manner—synthesized endless mounds of information generated by the exhibit and other sources into a crisp, readable text. Copies of this publication have grown very scarce, while the demand for it has increased.

In 1997, the Civil Liberties Public Education Fund, the body created by Congress to distribute funds to support projects that help educate the public about the Japanese American incarceration, provided a grant to enable the Wing Luke Asian Museum to republish an expanded version of the "Executive Order 9066" booklet.

I trust that this book, like *Executive Order 9066: 50 Years Before and 50 Years After,* the project that spawned it, will continue to enlighten future generations about the injustice of the incarceration, long after the Nisei, now in their senior years, have vanished from the scene. The story now passes into the hands of all of us, we who have an obligation to understand and remember.

Ron Chew
Executive Director
Wing Luke Asian Museum

AUTHOR'S PREFACE

Two weeks before the opening of the "Executive Order 9066" exhibit in February 1992, I was in a bit of a panic. I was finishing the writing of the captions and still hadn't identified some of the people in the photographs. Not to worry, one of the exhibit organizers assured me, we'll call in the Nisei. By midmorning, clusters of elderly men and women in winter coats and hats stood before various photos, pointing and reminiscing while we took notes. Some of them could recall the past more easily than others.

"Say, isn't that, ah, whatsizzname—Tamayo? I forget the first name. His sister Ruth was in my Japanese class."

"Didn't she go out with Herbert Katayama?"

"No, that was, ah, you know, Ruth *Wakai*."

"Yes, of course."

"Yeah, that's him all right. Bunzei. Bunzei Tamayo was his name."

No one, it seemed, could help us with one of the largest and most striking photographs, the one of a girl playing the violin. Dressed in an exquisite satin gown and silvery shoes, she was poised and serene, readying to play her first note. Her stern-looking teacher was seated to her left. She looked to be about 14 years old. I was resigned to a generic description until two days before the opening when she was identified as Kazuko Tajitsu, a child prodigy who went on to study at the Juilliard School of Music in New York.

A few months later, I was astonished when my mother, in Seattle on a visit from Hawaii, approached the very same photograph and exclaimed excitedly, "Kazu! That's Kazu!"

"You know her?"

"Yes! Yes! That's Kazu Ta-Ta-..."

"Tajitsu," I said.

"Tajitsu. Kazu Tajitsu. What a lovely person."

A native of Honolulu, my mother was attending fashion school in Los Angeles when the war broke out and was imprisoned in Manzanar, California. She left camp in January 1943 to attend a design school in New York City, where she eventually met the Tajitsu sisters, Terry and Kazuko. Kazuko, it turned out, introduced my mother to the Takami family, and my mother and father were married five years later.

I was thrilled. This, at long last, was my personal link to the exhibition and the Seattle Japanese community. The Sansei (third-generation Japanese Americans) on the committee all had direct ties; family photos and artifacts were used in the exhibition. When I thought about it later, however, I realized I already felt a strong connection to the history, having relived it in a sense during the year of research, interviews, and writing. A number of Nisei took me on a deeply personal journey into the past: Shig Ishikawa and Shigeko Uno conjured up the sights and sounds of my chief fascination, prewar Nihonmachi; Sharon Aburano, Cherry Kinoshita, and Tama Tokuda recalled the dark days before and after Pearl Harbor; Fumi and Ted Matsuda revived dusty images of Minidoka and southern Idaho.

By the time the exhibition opened, the Sansei, all of us born after the war, were in the habit of talking about *our* memories of Nihonmachi in the 1940s or camp life in Idaho. "You know, a cable car used to run up Yesler and down to Lake Washington," Shig would say, and I would nod and reply, "Yes, we remember that." And part of us did remember.

Now, six years later, my connection is even more direct, with the arrival of my sons, James and Robin, two Seattle-born Japanese Americans. And six years later, the history of this community is still emerging. The republishing of the catalog in book form has given me the opportunity to expand sections, especially the postwar period, and make clarifying corrections and additions. Where possible, I added short vignettes to help illustrate the history in human terms. The book also contains 28 additional photographs and graphics, most of them from the 1992 Wing Luke exhibition, but some of which have never before been shown or published.

A few words about terminology. I sometimes use the word "Nikkei," meaning persons of Japanese ancestry, for the sake of brevity. This obviates the need to continually describe my subjects as "Japanese and Japanese Americans."

After several edifying e-mail exchanges with historians Louis Fiset and Roger Daniels, and Japanese American National Museum curator Gary Kawaguchi, I decided to limit the use of the words "evacuation," "relocation," and "internment" in reference to the broad experience of the expulsion and imprisonment of Nikkei during World War II. I chose to use harsher but more accurate words such as "concentration camps," "inmates," "incarceration," and "imprisonment."

"Evacuation" was a government euphemism for the West Coast deracination of Japanese Americans, a word usually applied to the removal of citizens for their own safety in time of flood, landslide, or other imminent danger. "Internment" technically applies to prison camps run by the U.S. Justice Department for suspect Issei just after Pearl Harbor and to more permanent army-run camps for some of these detainees. The distinction is critical: the internment of enemy aliens during a war has a basis in law—specifically the Alien and Sedition Acts of 1798—and it is governed by international accord in the form of the Geneva Conventions. The roundup and incarceration of American citizens had no legal precedent and singled out a race of people. My purpose is not to quibble over words, but to get at the truth of what happened in plain, direct language.

I am indebted to a large number of friends, fellow researchers, and community members who generously shared with me their memories, both happy and painful, and their personal and professional expertise. Most of those people and organizations are listed in the acknowledgments at the end of the book, but I wanted to mention a few here.

Among those providing me with invaluable advice and direction on the overall text were Gary Iwamoto; Mayumi Tsutakawa; Louis Fiset; Cherry Kinoshita; Ken Mochizuki; Bob Shimabukuro; my wife, Wingate Packard; and Ed Suguro. Ed in particular was an inexhaustible source of community history, and he helped me track down information and tie up loose ends on numerous occasions.

The staff at the Wing Luke Asian Museum were also unfailingly helpful and professional. They included Ron Chew, Beth Takekawa, Charlene Mano, Kristi Woo, and Ruth Vincent.

I also want to recognize the phenomenal work of the "9066" exhibition committee back in 1992. Michelle Kumata, Sally Yamasaki, and the late Harry Fujita were the co-chairs who organized the exhibit, mobilizing a small army of community volunteers to research the history and collect artifacts and photographs. All three of them inspired me and taught me more than any book or library archive could have.

Most of all I want to thank the elders in the community, the generous and kind Nisei men and women who welcomed this ex–New Yorker into their hearts and homes and helped me envision the past. The experience remains among the most enriching and satisfying in my life.

David A. Takami, 1998

In memory of Harry Fujita, who touched us with his wit, wisdom, and gentle spirit

For James and Robin, the next generation

Painting by Hisashi Hagiya. Courtesy Yuki Miyake.

INTRODUCTION

HUNT, IDAHO, IS SITUATED on one of the great volcanic plains of the world, a vast expanse of land spreading toward low-lying mountains in the north and southwest and to rolling hills at the edge of the Snake River Valley.

Prior to the Second World War, much of the area was barren desert. The land was settled as a part of a federal homesteading project in the early 1900s, but by 1932, it was abandoned because of harsh conditions. An arid climate and forbidding terrain—layers of lava rock topped with powdery soil—combined to make the plains inhospitable to life other than a scattering of sagebrush, rattlesnakes, and scorpions.

It was here, more than 50 years ago, that the United States government imprisoned 9,700 first- and second-generation Japanese Americans for three years in a concentration camp called Minidoka.

In the weeks after Pearl Harbor, allegations of Japanese American disloyalty were investigated and largely disproved by the FBI and the U.S. Congress. Despite this knowledge, on February 19, 1942, President Franklin Roosevelt signed Executive Order 9066, setting in motion the expulsion of 110,000 people from the West Coast to 10 inland prison camps. At the time of their lockup, not one of these people was accused or convicted of any crime. No one was given due process of law as required by the U.S. Constitution. No Nikkei (person of Japanese ancestry) was charged with or convicted of any act of espionage or sabotage.

In the name of "military necessity," tens of thousands of people, two-thirds of them American citizens, were plucked from their homes, businesses, and neighborhoods, and made prisoners of war in their own country. They were presumed guilty because of their ancestry.

The future looked bleak and uncertain to Japanese Americans penned up on the dusty plains of Minidoka. In a few short weeks, the accomplishments of half a century were extinguished. Japanese immigrants, called Issei, had arrived on the West Coast of America trying to better their lives. At first, they worked on railroads, in sawmills, and in canneries, eking out a living and enduring relentless discrimination in immigration, employment, and housing. Others turned to farming, converting land covered with marshes and tree stumps into productive cropland. Hardships notwithstanding, they raised families, ran businesses, and developed a vibrant community life.

The beginning of World War II was the beginning of the end of the Japanese community in Seattle and in cities throughout the West Coast. "The evacuation was like a great fire that consumed much of [our] past," wrote Norio Mitsuoka of Seattle in his book *Nisei Odyssey*.

But even as the uprooting was destroying a way of life, a new life was emerging. While their parents and families languished in concentration camps, Nisei, second-generation Japanese Americans, joined the U.S. armed forces and served on the European and Pacific fronts. After the war, Japanese Americans enjoyed greater freedom and opportunities and began to enter the American mainstream. Energized by the civil rights movement, the third generation, or Sansei, worked with the Nisei to redress the injustice of the wartime imprisonment and waged new battles against discrimination and racism. Young people spurred renewed interest in their culture and heritage in America.

Replete with hardship, denial, and ruin, the history of Japanese America also resonates with resilience and triumph.

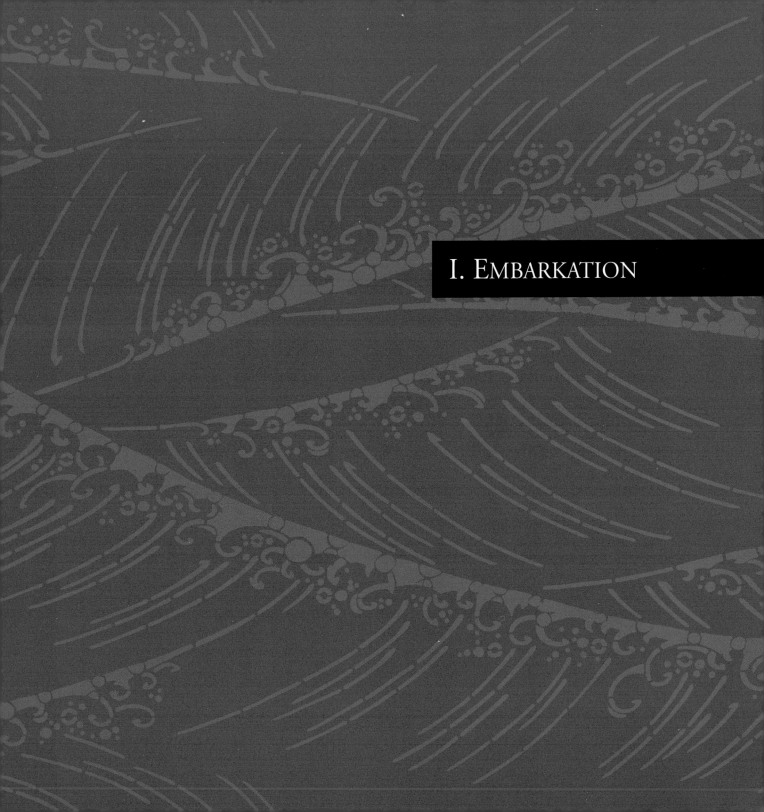

I. EMBARKATION

Chiyoko Shiromura (seated) and family, circa 1910. Courtesy Seattle Buddhist Temple Archives, Nakagawa Collection.

P A R T   O N E

EMBARKATION

COMING TO AMERICA

THE INTIMIDATING PRESENCE of Commodore Matthew Perry's well-armed black ships in Edo Bay signaled the end of Japan's 200 years of isolation from the West. It was 1853. The Tokugawa Shogunate was in its twilight, and the Americans negotiated trade and diplomatic treaties highly favorable to the U.S. In the ensuing 50 years, the Meiji Restoration brought about tumultuous social and economic change. Universal public education was instituted. Western ideas and influence profoundly affected the setup of the new government in Tokyo and the push toward industrialization.

The massive societal revolution took a toll on the large peasant class. Farmers were burdened by new national taxes and, in the early 1880s, a drastic drop in the price of rice. Thousands of farmers and peasants lost their homes and land.

Immigration seemed an attrac-tive option to many rural Japanese, who sought to work abroad for a few years, earn a great fortune, and return home to pay their debts.

Japanese first immigrated to Hawaii in 1868, the first year of Meiji. Once contract work was legalized by Japan in 1886, laborers began arriving in larger numbers. Large-scale immigration to the U.S. mainland from both Hawaii and Japan began in the 1890s and continued until 1924.

In the Pacific Northwest, as elsewhere in the West, the labor-intensive industries of mining, agriculture, logging, and railroad construction created an enormous demand for workers. When the Chinese Exclusion Act of 1882 cut off the supply of Chinese workers, Japanese labor filled the void. In Japan, shipowners and emigration companies recruited workers through ads in daily newspapers and painted a golden picture of America as a land of "money trees" with "gold, silver and gems...scattered on the streets." Impoverished, debt-ridden farmers were only too eager to believe.

The Oriental Trading Company of Seattle was among several brokers that recruited labor for major railroad companies in the Northwest, signing up workers from branch offices in Hiroshima and Wakayama. Young men came from all over the country, waiting for anywhere from a few days to several months at emigrant houses in the port cities of Yokohama and Kobe.

During the two-week voyage, hope often turned to despair. Passengers were squeezed into dark, damp holds of ships, enduring seasickness, lice-infested beds, poor ventilation, and nearly inedible food. "We were like silkworms on a tray, eating

Yasuhei Takekawa in 1920 when he returned to the U.S. from Japan with his wife, Kaneji. Passport courtesy Takekawa family.

Castaways, Stowaways

Despite an official Japanese prohibition on emigration for most of the 19th century, individual Japanese made it to the U.S. West Coast through enterprise or accident.

Three sailors were the first recorded Japanese to arrive in Washington state in December 1833. After 13 months adrift at sea, they landed on the Washington coast near Cape Flattery and stayed for a year at Fort Vancouver before leaving the U.S.

One of the first known Japanese in Seattle was Kyuhachi Nishii, who worked as a scullion aboard the U.S. steamer *Alexandria,* landing in Oregon, and then Seattle in the early 1880s. He jumped ship in 1884 and eventually found work at a sawmill at Port Blakely on Bainbridge Island, where he discovered that 30 or so Japanese were already employed. Mill officials didn't bother learning the names of Japanese workers who were known for payroll purposes as "Jap Number One," "Jap Number Two," etc. Nishii went on to open a restaurant in Seattle—the Star Cafe—in 1888.

and sleeping and wondering what the future held for us," recalled one Issei man.

Seattle and Tacoma were the major ports of entry on the Puget Sound. In Seattle, the steamships docked at Smith Cove at the north end of Elliott Bay. When the Japanese arrived, the city was still a relatively new settlement, rough at the edges. A fire destroyed a large portion of the downtown area in 1889, the same year that Washington Territory achieved statehood. Puget Sound tide flats covered most of the area south of downtown to the edge of Beacon Hill. Taking over Indian land, white settlers had begun to harvest the territory's abundance of natural resources to fuel rapidly expanding industries on the East Coast.

Pioneer Square was a bawdy, bustling home to loggers and sailors and, initially, to the new immigrants. Early Japanese arrivals included students, young men seeking to avoid the military draft, unemployed veterans of the Russo-Japanese War, and second- and third-born sons, who by Japanese law could not inherit land. Most of the Japanese immigrating to the Northwest came from rural regions in Hiroshima, Yamaguchi, and Okayama prefectures.

ON THE JOB

JOBS WERE PLENTIFUL on railroads and in sawmills, logging camps, and canneries. The immigrants

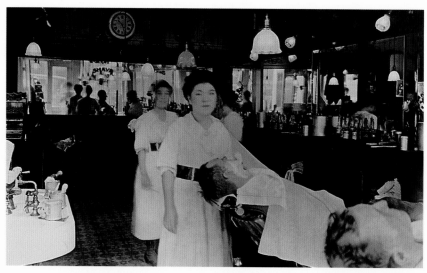

Mrs. Hatsune (Fukuda) Ikeda in the Fukuda Barber Shop, circa 1915. Courtesy Dr. S. Fukuda.

The T. Takayoshi Company in Port Blakely, Bainbridge Island, delivers food and supplies to Japanese families and workers, circa 1900. Courtesy Museum of History and Industry.

toiled long hours for paltry wages, nearly always lower than those for whites doing similar work. Seattle was a point of embarkation for jobs up and down the Pacific Coast and inland across the Cascade Mountains to eastern Washington, Idaho, and Montana.

Recruited by Tobo and Furuya and other companies, railroad workers put in grinding, 10-hour days on the Northern Pacific and Great Northern railroads, working as section hands and engine watchmen. Pay was low—from 85 cents to $1.50 per day—and workers tried to save money by cutting back on food expenses, subsisting on thin soup, rice, and mock soy sauce made from burned flour, sugar, salt, and water. Many suffered night blindness and other ailments from malnutrition. For amusement, the workers gambled, smoked cigarettes, and drank cheap whiskey. At night, they slept in temporary shacks or abandoned boxcars. Some Japanese worked in roundhouses and as redcap porters at Seattle's King Street Station.

By 1909, nearly 3,000 Japanese worked in Washington sawmills. Port Blakely on the southern tip of Bainbridge Island was the largest sawmill on the West Coast. Kunitaro Tanabe came to Washington state in 1917 to join his father who worked at the sawmill in Eatonville. "Although I was small, I was tough. But such heavy labor from the beginning soon made me feel completely washed out....I was completely discouraged. I hadn't known that America was a country where people had to work so hard just in order to eat."

Japanese began working in salmon canneries on Puget Sound and in Alaska as early as the late 1890s, relieving a shortage of Chinese workers. Cannery workers pitched, sorted, and gutted many thousands of fish on their 12-hour shifts. A sorter, for example, used large hooks in both hands to separate king salmon from sockeye. The butchers would then cut off heads, slit stomachs, and clean out the innards by hand. Despite numerous baths, the stench from a summer of standing in sweat, filth, and rotten fish entrails would sometimes last long after the season ended. Banned from most labor unions, Japanese did form a cannery workers' union in Seattle in 1936. Nisei Taul Watanabe, George Takegawa, and Dyke Miyagawa fought for and won higher wages and better working conditions for Japanese and Filipino workers. Issei were also instrumental in Northwest oyster production in several areas on Puget Sound.

Japanese who settled in the cities of Seattle and Tacoma included merchants, restaurateurs, domestic workers, doctors, and others with dubious backgrounds. An 1891 report by Japanese consular official

Worker on salmon barge in Alaska cannery, circa 1929. Courtesy NKHA Photo Collection.

Toshio Fujita estimated that of the 250 Japanese in Seattle, many of them were pimps, prostitutes, and gamblers. Frequently tricked or coerced into service by unscrupulous

Japanese railroad workers atop Great Northern Railroad cars, circa 1900. Courtesy Hanada Family Collection.

contractors, the women were smuggled into the country and worked in prostitution houses near King and Dearborn streets. Waka Yamada, a noted writer and critic in prewar Japan, was lured by tales of fabulous wealth, only to be forced into prostitution in Seattle under the name of "Oyae of Arabia."

Women were otherwise a rarity in early Japanese America. At the turn of the century, the ratio of men to women was 33 to 1. When Frank Natsuhara's mother first arrived in the U.S. in 1905, she was 20 years old and one of only a handful of women in the White River Valley, south of Seattle. "These young guys would love to come over and she'd make Japanese food," Natsuhara recounts. "They were homesick and some of them just wanted to watch a Japanese woman walk."

PIONEER FARMERS

MORE INDEPENDENT Japanese began farming land in outlying areas in King and Pierce counties, and in Yakima and Spokane. Near Seattle, Japanese truck farmers were centered in Bellevue, east of Lake Washington, and the White River and Puyallup valleys. The first Japanese settled in the White River Valley in 1893 and in Bellevue in 1898. Others farmed

Nishitani Oriental Gardens

Denjiro Nishitani's arrival in Seattle in 1906 was pure happenstance. Nishitani was heading by ship to San Francisco when news of the great earthquake in the Bay Area caused the ship's captain to head north and dock in Seattle. It didn't seem to matter to the 28-year-old Tottori Prefecture native, who hoped to earn a small fortune to help educate his four children back in Japan. America was America.

His first job was washing dishes in a restaurant. Soon afterward, he used skills learned on his family farm in Japan to find work as a farmhand. In 1908, he became a gardener for a wealthy family in Seattle's Green Lake neighborhood, and in 1912 he struck out on his own, leasing a five-acre site with a greenhouse a few miles to the north near what is now Lake City Way.

The area was sparsely populated and nearly wild stump land, with more than a few sightings of bears and cougars. Denjiro Nishitani, joined by his wife, Jin, and oldest son, Hiromu, developed the land into the renowned Oriental Gardens with park-like plantings of trees and shrubs, a nursery, and a retail florist shop that sold

The Nishitani family's Oriental Gardens, circa 1916. Courtesy Martha Nishitani.

geraniums, petunias, poinsettias, Easter lilies, and other seasonal plants.

By the 1920s, the three Nishitani children still living in Japan were brought to the U.S., joining Hiromu and their six American-born siblings. All of them helped out with the nursery and florist shop, and Hiromu took over the family business in 1926 after the death of his father.

During World War II, the Nishitanis were incarcerated in Minidoka, Idaho, while Hiromu's Caucasian wife and two sons stayed behind to run the gardens. The family sold the land in 1973, but many of the old trees and landscaping planted by Denjiro Nishitani remain today.

land near Green Lake, north of downtown Seattle, and on Vashon and Bainbridge islands in Puget Sound.

Many Japanese got their start as seasonal laborers working on area farms for a dollar a day in the summer and 80 cents a day in winter. The winter work typically was clearing land of marshes and huge tree stumps, which were removed by dynamiting and extracting the roots with large hooks pulled by

In the 1920s, Japanese farmers supplied 75 percent of the region's vegetables and half the milk.

horses. Uprooting and burning a single large stump could take up to a month, and the entire process could consume several years. American landowners benefited greatly from the conversion to productive farmland at a minimal cost, and some rewarded Japanese workers with reduced rents, enabling them to start farms.

The farms were small, averaging 5 to 15 acres, but successful because of the farmers' advanced knowledge of fertilization, irrigation, and cultivation. They also worked cooperatively, helping one another build homes and raise money through *tanomoshi* clubs that lent money to members on a rotating basis. Seeding, thinning, transplanting, weeding, dusting, and spraying were all done by hand.

More than half of all Japanese farms in Washington state were located in the White River Valley. The Valley's loamy, sandy soil was ideal for growing berries and other crops such as lettuce, beans, cauliflower, peas, cabbage, celery, carrots, radishes—almost any vegetable in demand. Greenhouses also sprang up in the Valley and north Seattle. While dairy and berry farmers joined organizations to help them market and sell their products, vegetable growers were on their own. Japanese truck farmers sold their produce at the Pike Place Market starting in 1912, five years after the market was founded. By the beginning of World War I, they occupied a staggering 70 percent of market stalls. In the 1920s, by some estimates, Japanese supplied 75 percent of the region's vegetables and half the milk. Japanese-run dairies, most of them in the White River Valley, flourished until the price of milk declined in the late 1920s.

The Kato, Hanada, and Miyoshi families pick berries, 1918. Courtesy Mae Iseri Yamada.

Japanese farmers sell produce at the Pike Place Market, circa 1910. Courtesy Museum of History and Industry, Webster/Stevens Collection.

In Bellevue, the Japanese cleared and settled hundreds of acres of land at and around the center of what is now the city's downtown area. Where shopping malls and office buildings stand today, immigrants grew strawberries and vegetables and worked at a local sawmill.

Life on the farm was primitive at first. Few farms had electricity or running water, and workdays were long and exhausting. Kimiko Ono, the wife of a Renton truck farmer, described her day:

"At around 6:30 a.m. I prepared breakfast, awakened the children and all the family sat down at the breakfast table together. Then my husband took the tomatoes to Pike Market.

"I watered the plants in the green-houses, taking the three children along with me. During the daytime I took care of the tomatoes outside.... I worked continually. My husband came back at 7 p.m. and I worked

Mrs. Shiki Harui and Mrs. Hatsuno Seko with large chrysanthemums on Bainbridge Island, circa 1920. Courtesy BIJAC Archives.

with him for a while...then I sorted the tomatoes which I had picked in the morning and put them into boxes. When I was finally through with the boxing, it was midnight if I finished early or 1:30 if I did not."

Typically the whole family pitched in on the farm, with women and children picking vegetables and fruit and the men doing the heavy field work.

At the peak of Japanese farming in 1920, more than 1,000 Japanese cultivated 25,000 acres in the state, more than double the land farmed by Japanese in 1910.

ROOTS OF RACISM

FROM THEIR ARRIVAL in the United States, Japanese, like other Asians on the West Coast, faced blatant racial hatred and discrimination. On the U.S. mainland, the number of Japanese rose rapidly from 2,039 in 1890 to 24,326 in 1900 to 72,157 in 1910. As the white mainstream felt the growing economic competition, their resentment and prejudice grew.

By law, Japanese could not own land, live in certain areas, or become naturalized U.S. citizens. Racial covenants against renting or selling homes to Japanese were written into real estate contracts in West Seattle, Magnolia, and other Seattle

The Kiichiro Hamamoto family in front of their family farm in South Park, circa 1933. Courtesy Seattle Buddhist Temple Archives, Henry and Yuki Miyake Collection.

neighborhoods. De facto segregation existed in public schools. Japanese were made to sit in balconies at theaters, refused admittance to the Alki Natatorium, Golden Gardens Beach, and the Crystal Pool, and insulted by epithets such as "dogfish" and "goddamn Jap!"

As the Nisei reached employment age, college graduates with professional degrees couldn't find work in the white community and settled for jobs as bellhops, grocery clerks, gardeners, dishwashers, and truck drivers.

Anti-Japanese agitation centered in California, where Japanese were most numerous, but similar movements began in the Northwest. Racism against Asians was hardly a new phenomenon in western Washington. The Chinese experienced the wrath of the white community when they were driven out of Seattle and Tacoma by mob violence in the mid-1880s. In April 1900, the King County Republican Club called for the exclusion of Japanese, citing the "menace to the conditions which make it possible for the intelligent

· 23 ·

American working man to maintain himself, his family and his home."

About the same time, a public uproar ensued in the White River Valley when Japanese workers replaced white children who had been loafing on the job on a farm in Kent. Recalled one farmworker, "After that trouble, it was dangerous for us to go into Kent because we were targets for jeers, sticks and stones whenever we appeared on the streets." Racial animosity toward the Japanese built steadily throughout the early part of the century. In 1908, Japan agreed to stop issuing passports to laborers in exchange for the United States rescinding an order to segregate Japanese students in San Francisco. This became known as the Gentlemen's Agreement. The U.S. government completely cut off immigration from Japan with the signing of the Immigration Act of 1924.

Before they had been in the country for a decade, Japanese were criticized as "unassimilable," and politicians and newspapermen issued dire warnings of the "mongrelization" of the white race. Among the leading hate-mongers was William Randolph Hearst, whose papers, including the *Seattle Post-Intelligencer*, were notorious for their anti-Japanese propaganda. One Hearst paper, the *New York American*, published the following poem in its July 23, 1916, edition:

HYMN OF HATE

They've battleships, they say,
On Magdelena Bay!
Uncle Sam, won't you listen when
we warn you?
They meet us with a smile
But they're working all the while
And they're waiting just to steal our
California!
So just keep your eyes on Togo,
With his pockets full of maps,
For we've found out we can't trust
the Japs!

In 1919, Seattle businessmen formed the Anti-Japanese League. White farmers and businessmen clearly feared the competition. "They are not inferior to us," said League President Miller Freeman in 1920. "In fact, they constantly demonstrate their ability to best the white man at his own game in farming, fishing and business. They will work harder, deprive themselves of every comfort and luxury, make beasts of burden of their women and stick together, making a combination that America cannot defeat."

The racists singled out Japanese farmers in particular. The Washington State Legislature passed the Alien Land Law in 1921, on the heels of a similar law in California. Washington's 1889 constitution, in fact, banned the sale of land to "aliens ineligible in citizenship" (only Asians were ineligible to become naturalized U.S. citizens); the new law extended the restrictions to cover leasing or renting land and renewing old leases.

Issei farmers got around the law by making arrangements with white farmers, who would technically own the land and employ the Japanese as "managers." Because these were verbal agreements, however, some Japanese lost their land in subsequent property disputes. Issei also bought land in the names of their children, who were American citizens by virtue of being born in the U.S., or other older Nisei, but that loophole was closed by a 1923 amendment to the land law.

After 1921, Japanese farmers lived in constant fear of losing their property and livelihood. Sashiro and Rin Hasabe had leased 15 acres of land in the Green Lake area and invested $5,000 in greenhouses. After the law went into effect, the legal owners declared their verbal agreement void and evicted them from the land.

"I don't know how to earn a living [after the law passes]," said one Issei farmer from O'Brien in the White River Valley. "An old man is not wanted for railroad or sawmill work and city life is too strenuous for me....This law has deprived me and my family of my natural right to find happiness by honest work."

Total Japanese-owned land in the White River Valley was reduced by thousands of acres. Yet by 1942,

Japanese still farmed about 56 percent of all agricultural land in King County.

MAIN STREET (NIHONMACHI), U.S.A.

THE REAL ESTATE covenants and employment discrimination had the effect of creating a large and lively ghetto in the south end of downtown Seattle, called Nihonmachi or Japantown.

The origins of Nihonmachi go back to 1891, when a city map showed that Dearborn Street was then called "Mikado Street." In the ensuing years, more Japanese moved from Pioneer Square on the waterfront to the east along Jackson and Yesler, especially after Jackson Street was regraded in 1908.

Nihonmachi grew and prospered. On weekends, laborers flocked to the district for baths, haircuts, and entertainment, chiefly gambling and prostitution. The Toyo Club, located in the building where the Bush Garden Restaurant now stands, was the second largest gambling house on the West Coast. Founded in 1920, the club ran blackjack and Chinese gambling games in three large rooms on the second floor. The club was equipped with a silent alarm at the cigarette stand on the first floor, which warned patrons of impending police raids.

S.K. Kanada, a representative of the Japanese government, cataloged businesses in the Seattle Japanese community in a 1908 magazine article. These included restaurants, barbershops, bathhouses, laundries, hotels and lodging houses, groceries, bakeries, meat and fish markets, Japanese general merchandise stores, tailors, dentists, physicians, interpreters, and cigar and candy stores.

By the mid-1920s, trade with Japan and Asia was booming, accounting for well over half the value of exports and imports at the Port of Seattle. Down on the waterfront, as many as 35 Japanese businesses operated to handle the trade. The biggest and most successful Japanese business was the Furuya Company on 2nd Avenue in downtown Seattle. Founded by Masajiro Furuya in 1892, it was a one-stop multipurpose business that provided services in real estate, construction, mailing, printing, and banking in addition to selling food, sake, and gifts from Japan. Traveling salesmen from Furuya hawked their wares to Japanese laborers living in work camps in Washington state and as far away as Idaho, Montana, and

The Yamatoya dry goods store on Jackson Street, circa 1910. Courtesy Museum of History and Industry, Webster/Stevens Collection.

Wyoming. When the company went bankrupt in the fall of 1931, many Japanese lost their life savings, land, and businesses.

Into the 1920s and 1930s, more families set up small businesses in Nihonmachi. In many ways it was like a small town. Everyone knew everyone else. Yukiko Miyake (née Hirata) recalls coming home from school one day: "One of the boys from my school—he was a senior and I was a freshman—bought me an ice cream cone. We walked three to four blocks and by the time I got home, my grandma knew all about it. That's how fast gossip traveled around there."

Shig Ishikawa was born in the heart of Nihonmachi in the Sun Hotel on Main Street between 5th and 6th avenues. His father leased the hotel that housed itinerant Japanese and Filipino workers. Down the street was the popular Chinese restaurant, Gyokko-ken Cafe. State Drug Store was at 5th and Main, and around the corner were the offices of the *Japanese American Courier* newspaper. The neighborhood was always busy, especially on weekends, when farmers and laborers would come into town from the countryside.

Growing up in Nihonmachi in the 1920s provided a wonderful blend of Japan and America. After school, Shig and his friends would roam the alleys and sidewalks, shoot-

> The smells of *soba* broth, *shoyu,* and other Japanese foods wafted through the air. Passersby spoke Japanese. After dark, men strolled about in *yukata* and *geta* (wooden slippers) to the strains of *shamisen* from nearby restaurants or music schools.

ing marbles, flipping milk-bottle tops, or playing *jintori,* a Japanese tag game played between two telephone poles. Japanese food was plentiful, but the boys often preferred hot dogs and baloney sandwiches for lunch. In the summer, they frequented the confection store Sagamiya, buying snacks such as *senbei* (rice crackers) and *kintoki* (shaved ice with beans and syrup), and played baseball on a vacant lot south of Weller along 5th. For 10 cents they could watch the latest Rin Tin Tin movie at the Atlas Theater on Maynard Avenue.

The center of Nihonmachi was 6th and Main. During the *bon odori* festival, a bandstand for musicians was constructed in the blocked-off intersection. Main Street from 5th to Maynard was closed for the dancing, and shop owners hung colorful Japanese lanterns outside their doors. At other times of the year, the neighborhood could have been any town in Japan. The smells of *soba* broth, *shoyu,* and other Japanese foods wafted through the air. Passersby spoke Japanese. After dark, men strolled about in *yukata* and *geta* (wooden slippers) to the strains of *shamisen* from nearby restaurants or music schools.

On weekdays, Nihonmachi was filled with the sounds of delivery trucks stopping and starting, bells clanging, and train wheels on tracks. Toward the waterfront, steam billowed from trains pulling out of King Street Station. Interurban trolley cars ran from the terminus at Occidental and Main to Everett and Tacoma, while the Rainier Valley Line ran to Renton through 4th and Jackson. Just to the north on Yesler, one could ride a cable car all the way to Leschi Park on Lake Washington.

One of the most serene pleasures for hardworking Japanese of all ages was the public bath. Many Japanese lived in hotels without bathing facilities. For 15 cents, Japanese could take a bath at one of eight or so Japanese-style public

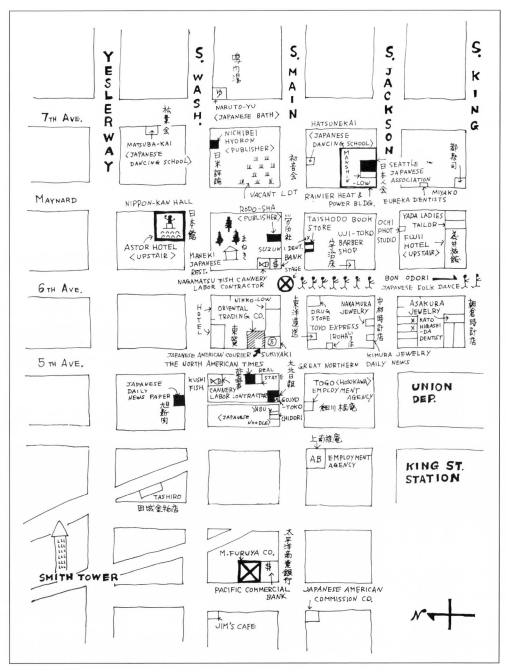

Map of Nihonmachi in the 1920s. From Kazuo Ito's Issei.

Higo 10 Cents Store

In the heyday of Nihonmachi in the 1930s, a penny could buy a handful of candy, trolley tokens were two for a nickel, and a dime—a whole dime—could buy you any number of household goods at the Higo 10 Cents Store.

The store was already a fixture in the neighborhood in 1932, when Sanzo Murakami moved his business from its old location in a storefront on the ground floor of the Presley Hotel at 7th Avenue and Weller Street to a new building he constructed on Jackson Street.

Jackson was the main thoroughfare through Japantown, with trolleys running up and down the street and all of the hustle and bustle of the mostly Japanese immigrant families who lived and worked in the neighborhood. On weekends, the population ballooned with the arrival of farmers and laborers who worked in outlying areas around Seattle proper.

Masa and Aya Murakami, the two sisters who run the business today, recall those early days with fondness. "It sure was *nigiyaka* [lively]," says Masa, who helped their father after school and on weekends. The store became an informal gathering spot for natives of Kumamoto Prefecture, where Sanzo Murakami had been born and raised in the city of Higo. Masa remembers the loud, warmhearted Kumamoto farmers who frequently brought her family gifts of lettuce and celery and other vegetables.

The store sold enamel tea kettles, pots and pans, kitchen utensils, stove pipes for potbellied stoves, *tabi* for farmers, *geta,* Japanese toys, and fabric for western and Japanese clothing—among hundreds of other items.

During the war, the store was boarded up (see photograph on page 48) and taken care of by one of the Murakamis' tenants while the family was imprisoned in Minidoka, Idaho. Eight days after they returned to Seattle in 1945, Sanzo Murakami passed away, and his wife and children took over the business. Today, the Murakami sisters run the store in the same Jackson Street location. The business was renamed the Higo Variety Store when the building was remodeled in 1957.

baths in Nihonmachi, including Hashidate-yu, Hinode-yu, Momiji-yu, and Miyako-yu. Bathers were given a bath towel, washcloth, and pail, and washed themselves with soap, then rinsed off before soaking in the hot tubs.

If there was a community center, it was the Nippon Kan Theater. Built with community funds in 1909, the Nippon Kan was busy several nights a week with actors and musicians from Japan, *kabuki,* movies, concerts, variety shows, *judo* and *kendo* competitions, and community meetings. In the early days, the theater was the site for important political debates. Famed Japanese soprano Tamaki Miura was among the honored performers, as was Eurasian tenor Yoshie Fujiwara.

Rise Yamasaki, with baby Yaiko, Tani Hayashida, with baby Marge, Teruko Sata, with her baby, and Mae (Hayashida) Ondo near Union Station, circa 1915. Courtesy Frank Yamasaki.

A night out at the Nippon Kan was a welcome diversion from the rigors of work and school. Most of the entertainers were delightfully unprofessional, sometimes forgetting their lines and struggling to improvise. Between performances, children ran up and down the balcony staircases and their parents caught up on the latest community gossip.

By the mid-1920s, Nihonmachi extended from 4th along Main to 7th, with clusters of businesses along Jackson, King, Weller, Lane, and Dearborn streets.

Among the major businesses were the Taiheiyo Sweater Knitting Mill near Maynard and Jackson, the Pacific Commercial Bank, the White River Dairy, and the Cascade Soda Water Company. In 1913, Shoichi Okamura founded the Grand Union Laundry, which became one of the largest employers in the community with 70 workers, including delivery men, washers, and dry cleaners.

As early as 1900, there were six Japanese-operated hotels in Seattle. At the Fujii Hotel at 5th and Jackson, laborers paid 25 cents a night for a room. Visiting Japanese dignitaries usually stayed at the fancier Northern Pacific (N.P.) Hotel on 6th. By 1925, there were 127 Japanese-managed hotels. Husband-and-wife proprietors worked day and night to clean lobbies and rooms, make the beds, and do the laundry.

The Grand Union Laundry near 14th Avenue on Main Street, circa 1913. Courtesy Frank Okamura, NKHA Photo Collection.

Lotus Buddhist Youth Club Entertainment performs at the Nippon Kan, circa 1936. Courtesy Seattle Buddhist Temple Archives, Henry and Yuki Miyake Collection.

Bon odori *festival in front of Seattle Buddhist Temple, August 1932. Courtesy Seattle Buddhist Temple Archives.*

The district began declining slightly in the early 1930s with the bad economic times. But by the end of the decade, Japanese were still an impressive economic force in Seattle. In 1940, Japanese comprised just 2 percent of the population in Seattle, yet they operated 50 greenhouses (63 percent of the city total), 206 hotels and 56 apartments (63 percent of the total), 225 restaurants (45 percent), 90 dry cleaning shops (23 percent), and 140 groceries (17 percent).

Smaller Japanese communities flourished in nearby Tacoma, with 90 Japanese residents in 1890, Port Blakely, Auburn, Yakima, and Spokane.

Cherry Land Florist on Jackson Street, circa 1940. Courtesy Seattle Buddhist Temple Archives, Henry and Yuki Miyake Collection.

GROWTH OF COMMUNITY LIFE

A RATHER LARGE LOOPHOLE in the 1908 Gentlemen's Agreement allowed for the immigration of wives and families and enabled community life to blossom. Men frequently wed "picture brides" from their home villages in marriages that were arranged by their parents and, after an exchange of photographs and family histories, were carried out by proxy in Japan. The women arrived in the U.S. clutching photographs of their husbands-to-be. Some were bitterly

Jefferson Laundry, circa 1910. Courtesy Hashimoto Family Collection.

Funeral in front of Seattle Buddhist Church, 1926. Courtesy Hashimoto Family Collection.

disappointed upon meeting the balding, shabbily dressed men who didn't look anything like their pictures or who had perhaps lied about their professions. Because the U.S. government didn't recognize the legality of such weddings until 1917, group marriage ceremonies were conducted in immigration offices. Japan cut off the flow of picture brides in 1920, under pressure from the United States.

In 1920, a quarter of Seattle's 7,874 Japanese had been born in this country; by 1930, nearly half were native born and the population grew to 8,448. Families began moving east and south of Nihonmachi.

Although some women worked on their own as seamstresses or maids, most became instant unpaid employees, working beside their husbands in stores, hotels, restaurants, and fields. Others worked as midwives, sometimes traveling great distances to deliver babies in outlying areas at a time when most children were born at home.

Women and children gave community life a new dimension. Work was paramount, but on weekends and holidays, Japanese found many ways to enjoy life. Japanese customs and cuisine took on new meaning in the American setting. Jefferson Park on Beacon Hill was the site of many a Nihongo Gakko (Japanese Language School) picnic. People turned out in their best clothing and with a hearty appetite for a full day of fun, food, and baseball. Girls and boys practiced for months in advance for picnic performances of folk dances, songs, marching drills, and mass calisthenics. Japanese holidays, *Oshogatsu* (New Year's), Boys' Day, and Girls' Day were celebrated along with Christmas, Thanksgiving, and the Fourth of July.

The Kinimoto family in front of Jim's Cafe in Pioneer Square, circa 1930. Courtesy Aki Kurose.

As in the surrounding white community, Seattle Japanese community life centered around school and church. Most Japanese children attended the old South School (renamed Main Street School) at 6th and Main in Nihonmachi, and later, nearby Bailey Gatzert School. They went on to Broadway, Garfield, or Franklin high schools. Nisei studied hard, some of them becoming star pupils and even class valedictorians.

Nearly 2,000 students attended Nihongo Gakko at its peak, studying two hours a day, five days a week, after regular school. Originally located on the second floor of the Furuya building on 2nd Avenue in 1902, the school moved to the

"Picture bride" Yeki Chikamura (née Osugi), circa 1914. Courtesy Amy Kobayashi.

Issei members of the Bailey Gatzert English class, circa 1920. Courtesy Hanada Family Collection.

Child prodigy Kazuko Tajitsu takes a violin lesson, circa 1937. Courtesy Seattle Buddhist Temple Archives, Henry and Yuki Miyake Collection.

prefecture. In Seattle, the largest of these were Hiroshima, Okayama, and Yamaguchi *kenjinkai*. Besides serving as social organizations, *kenjinkai* took care of members in need of money, housing, or employment, and generally helped ease the adjustment for newly arriving immigrants.

Of the larger community-wide organizations, the most prominent were the Nihonjinkai, or Japanese Association, and the Japanese Chamber of Commerce. Founded in 1900, the Nihonjinkai spoke out against discriminatory legislation while promoting Japanese businesses and community groups.

After school and on weekends, Nisei youngsters converged on Collins Playfield, across the street from the Buddhist Church, to play softball, football, and basketball. Baseball was especially popular among Nisei. Fierce but friendly rivalries developed among teams

Nisei undergraduates gather outside Suzzallo Library at the University of Washington, 1939. Shosuke Sasaki photo.

Buddhist Church before relocating in 1913 to its current location on 15th and Weller.

From the earliest days, churches were part of the foundation of the Japanese community in Seattle, helping to acculturate immigrants by teaching them English and finding them jobs. As the number of immigrants grew, so did the churches.

The Reverend Fukumatsu Okazaki helped found the Japanese Baptist Church in 1899. Soon, Methodist, Presbyterian, Episcopal, Catholic, and Congregational churches were formed, as was the Seattle Buddhist Church.

Most Japanese also belonged to *kenjinkai*, organizations of people from the same Japanese *ken*, or like Taiyo, Waseda, and the Nippon Athletic Club, and in leagues sponsored by the *Japanese American Courier* newspaper. Perhaps the most accomplished individual ballplayer was Joichi (Joe) Kesamaru, who starred at Broadway High School in 1931 and 1932 when the team won two city championships. Nisei boys also took *judo* and *kendo* lessons.

Schoolboy pitcher Susumu Shimokan, circa 1938. Courtesy Kats Iwamura.

Shibai

Before the war, theater performances at the Nippon Kan were the highlight of community entertainment. "In those days, there was no TV or bowling so this was our chief pleasure," recalls Kiki Hagimori.

Shibai (drama) was especially popular. Geijitsukyokai was the first drama club to be developed in 1920, followed soon after by the Buddhist Church's Lotus Entertainment, JACL Entertainment, and the Ginsei Club Entertainment.

Misters Hayashi and Ohashi were the main organizers and actors in Geijitsukyokai, which performed at the Nippon Kan once a year, usually in April.

The *shibai* were rarely famous plays, but rather ones that someone had happened to receive from Japan. Many Nisei, who didn't know Japanese very well, remember the arduous process of memorizing lines in Japanese.

Yukiko Miyake was a member of Lotus Entertainment. "It was a lot of fun. You'd have to memorize your lines and sometimes you'd forget, but when you were with a bunch of friends, you didn't care."

"When I was 13 years old, I played a woman in her 80s," recalls Kiki Hagimori. "I remember T. R. [Goto] saying that it was really amazing to see the transformation. It was...the challenge of what you could do. That's what I liked."

Practice for *shibai* was held five nights a week. Sometimes the children would stay up till midnight waiting their turn to rehearse their lines. Performances were generally from 7:30 to 10:30 P.M. During intermission, people would spread out the food they had brought like a picnic.

Other popular traditional arts of the day were *odori* (Japanese dance), *koto*, *shamisen*, and *shigin*, a kind of poetry singing.

After the war, *shibai* made way for *kabuki*. When Geijitsukyokai disbanded, the Buddhist Church purchased all the costumes and props.

Founded by James Sakamoto, the *Japanese American Courier* was the first English-language Japanese American newspaper in the country. Sakamoto was a colorful and controversial figure in the Seattle Nikkei community. A graduate of Franklin High School, he played semipro baseball and became a professional boxer in New York. In 1927, he returned to Seattle, blind from injuries to his eyes, and began the *Courier* the following year. He also helped establish the Japanese American Citizens League (JACL), serving as the organization's second national president.

The *Courier* joined established Japanese language dailies *Taihoku*

The 24-0 Langendorf basketball team, 1939. Front row: Francis "Bako" Kinoshita, Augustine "Augie" Aratani, Junie Kawamura, Jim Taro Takisaki; back row: "Squeeky" Kanazawa, John "Gooch" Kawaguchi, Yowge Yoshino, Sam Sakai, George Kosaka, Yutaka "Dutch" Takekawa. Courtesy Seattle Buddhist Temple Archives, Henry and Yuki Miyake Collection.

Bellevue Seinenkai girls' basketball team, 1930. Front row: Nobuko Inatsu, Kikuya Hirotaka, Tomoko Inatsu; back row: Sueko Yamaguchi, Mitsi Shiraishi, Mary Aramaki. Courtesy Cano Numoto.

Nippo and *Hokubei Jiji*, both of which carried sections in English.

Japanese artists enriched the cultural life of the community and made a significant impact on the emerging Seattle art world. In the 1930s, a loose association of notable painters known as the Group of Twelve included three Japanese, Takuichi Fujii, Kenjiro Nomura, and Kamekichi Tokita, who all painted Seattle city scenes in the gritty social realist style. Nomura and Tokita ran the Noto Sign Company in Nihonmachi as a way to make a living. Photographer Kyo Koike, a physician by profession, achieved international acclaim with his "pictorialist" prints of nature.

As Nisei reached adulthood, they realized the future of the Japanese community depended on overcoming discrimination and pursuing an education. The Seattle Progressive Citizens League, a precursor of the JACL, was formed in 1921. The JACL held its first national convention in Seattle in August 1930.

Nisei also yearned to join the "melting pot" and become "100 percent American," a tendency reinforced by a sizable generation gap with the Issei, many of whom had married and had children late. Nisei were wild about Gary Cooper, Myrna Loy, the Andrews Sisters, Lou Gehrig,

The Amano family and Mr. Mimbu at a family picnic, October 1921. Courtesy Amano Family Collection.

Mochitsuki *(rice pounding) on New Year's Day in White River Valley, 1916. Courtesy George Yasumura.*

politics; they were too busy making a living and raising families. Many Nisei, on the other hand, were pro-American. Caught in the middle were the Kibei, Nisei who were educated in Japan, who saw both sides of the rift and believed they could bridge the growing misunderstandings.

The American public had long been exposed to news of Japanese troops in China and their growing ambitions to colonize much of Asia. Buck-toothed simian caricatures of the Japanese invaders appeared regularly in the national press after the Manchurian invasion of 1931. The talk of war intensified after the U.S. and other countries imposed economic embargoes on Japan beginning in late 1940.

Margaret (Nomura) Yamaguchi, Eunice Nakamura, Kiku (Shiraishi) Tatsumi, and Hanae (Yamada) Matsuda pose at Playland amusement park, circa 1939. Courtesy Hanae Matsuda.

Joe Louis, and Flash Gordon. Young women wore saddle shoes and bobby socks, wide-collared blouses, and gently waved hair. Boys dressed in loose suits with wide, cuffed trousers. Youngsters joined the Boy Scouts and Girl Scouts, school debating teams, and dance bands.

The abandonment of Japanese culture was disturbing to many in the older generation. "In any way they could become more like a white man, they thought that was progress," says Shosuke Sasaki, a younger Issei. "I eventually discovered that there were some Nisei girls who took great pride in the fact that they had lost their taste for soy sauce....I used to laugh at them and say, 'You'll never get rid of the color of your skin or the shape of your eyes. No matter how white you think you've become, you're always an imitation white.' They didn't like that at all."

The two generations reacted differently to the approach of World War II. Some Issei sympathized with Japanese militarism, having received the bulk of their information from Japanese-language newspapers, but most were detached from world

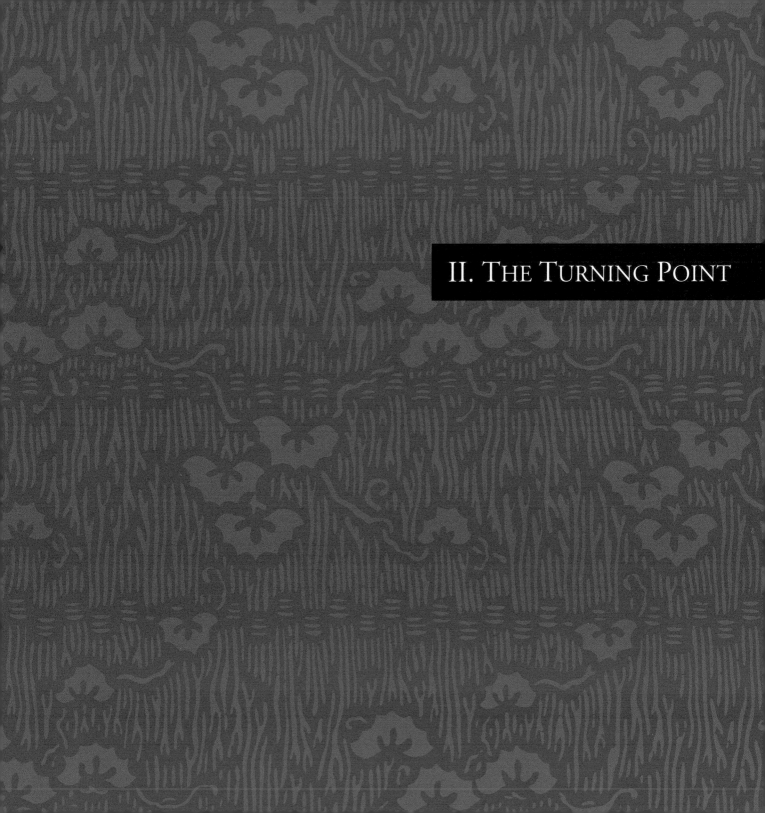

II. The Turning Point

Children alongside barracks in Minidoka, circa 1943. Courtesy Wing Luke Asian Museum, Hatate Family Collection.

P A R T T W O

THE TURNING POINT

DECEMBER 7 AND THE DAYS OF INFAMY

RACISM BY ITS very nature breeds in a swamp of ignorance and contradiction.

A week after the bombing of Pearl Harbor, President Roosevelt was moved to orate on the 150th anniversary of the signing of the Bill of Rights: "We will not, under any threat, or in the face of danger, surrender the guarantees of liberty our forefathers framed for us in our Bill of Rights." A little more than two months later, the president signed the executive order that set in motion what legal scholars have called the worst violation of constitutional rights in the nation's history. In the process, the government systematically destroyed the vibrant and productive Japanese American communities on the U.S. West Coast.

There can be no exaggerating the shock of Pearl Harbor on the Japanese in America. As other Americans exploded with anger and indignation at the news, the Japanese American community reacted with dread and foreboding.

Nobue Shimizu of Seattle was addressing Christmas cards when she heard the news. "It was the worst feeling I had in my whole life," she says. "But it had been coming. We knew because of the economic boycott. We read the papers and because of all the 'Jap this' and 'Japs that' you read in the newspapers, we knew [war] was coming, but when it did come, it left a sinking feeling in the pit of your stomach."

"Tonight our family had a conference," wrote an 18-year-old Nisei from Seattle in his diary on the night of December 9. "We talked about the future. Mother and father told us about Buddhism. She said now that our future on this earth looks dim—our main future lies in heaven, where we all must go."

Confusion reigned in the minds of the American-born Nisei. Many reacted by embracing their upbringing and rejecting their heritage. Wrote Monica Sone in *Nisei Daughter,* an evocative memoir of her childhood in Seattle: "An old wound opened up again, and I found myself shrinking inwardly from my Japanese blood, the blood of an enemy. I knew instinctively that the fact that I was an American by birthright was not going to help me escape the consequences of this unhappy war." The Sones and many other Japanese burned or discarded any evidence of a connection to Japan, such as Japanese flags, swords, language books, toys, and records.

The U.S. government wasted no time in clamping down on the community. For years before the war, government agents had been surveilling "suspect" Japanese, and in the months before Pearl Harbor, the War and Justice departments prepared for their apprehension. On that Sunday evening of December 7, the FBI began to arrest Issei and a few Nisei, including Buddhist priests, Japanese-language teachers, and others, who, as officials of community organizations, were considered potential spies. FBI agents came to the home of Jim Akutsu two days after Pearl Harbor. "They were pretty rough. They went through the house and took a radio, knives, binoculars...six inches of Indian pennies in a gallon jug." They also took away his father. Most Issei were taken to the jail at the Immigration and Naturalization Service building just south of Nihonmachi.

In subsequent days, Japanese were ordered to stay away from railroad tunnels, highway bridges, and radio stations. Travel was restricted. Issei business licenses were revoked and bank accounts were frozen.

By the middle of March 1942, 264 Seattle Issei had been arrested and sent to detention centers run by the U.S. Justice Department. Most went to Fort Missoula, Montana. They were separated from their families for months, even years.

On the U.S. West Coast, hatred of Japan was aimed at local Nikkei—despite the fact that the citizen Nisei comprised two-thirds of the Japanese community. Like millions of other Americans, Nisei rushed to join the army, buy war bonds, and donate blood. But the community was helpless in the face of growing hysteria. The seeds for the incarceration were planted on December 15, 1941, when Secretary of the Navy Frank Knox falsely accused Nikkei living in Hawaii of aiding

the "surprise" attack and implied the presence of a large espionage network.

Newspapers and politicians in the Seattle area at first urged restraint, professing trust of Nikkei neighbors, but the mood quickly turned hostile in early 1942 when American war losses mounted in the Pacific. The push to expel the

> Earl Warren, the future U.S. Supreme Court chief justice, asserted that the *absence* of Japanese "fifth column" activity on the West Coast was evidence that they were secretly planning another attack.

Japanese was centered in California. In many ways, the antagonism was a continuation of nearly a century of racial hate and exclusion campaigns, first against the Chinese and then the Japanese. Austin Anson, secretary-manager of the Grower-Shipper Association in Salinas, among others, lobbied for the exclusion in Washington, D.C., in the

spring of 1942. He explained his position with chilling honesty in an article in the *Saturday Evening Post:* "We're charged with wanting to get rid of the Japs for selfish reasons, and we might as well be honest. We do. It's a question of whether the white man lives on the Pacific Coast or the brown men."

California state attorney general Earl Warren, the future U.S. Supreme Court chief justice, was among those who asserted that the *absence* of Japanese "fifth column" activity on the West Coast was evidence that they were secretly planning another attack.

In Washington, D.C., Secretary of War Henry Stimson, Assistant Secretary of War John J. McCloy, and President Roosevelt himself were easily convinced by these arguments. One of the few high-ranking officials to oppose the exclusion, and one who was in a position to know the evidence, was FBI director J. Edgar Hoover. The decision to forcibly remove Japanese and Japanese Americans, said Hoover, was "based primarily on public and political pressures rather than factual data."

In Seattle, local Nikkei began to feel the heat. At King Street Station, Japanese redcap porters were replaced by Filipinos wearing large identification buttons reading "Filipino." In early 1942, 26 Nisei women clerks at Seattle public elementary schools resigned under pressure, after the school district received complaints from parents. City residents were divided over the resignations. A thousand University of Washington students signed a petition calling for their reinstatement, and one writer, in a letter to the editor of the *Seattle Post-Intelligencer,* pleaded with school authorities "not to yield to the sentiments of race prejudice." Mrs. Esther M. Sekor, chairman of the Gatewood Elementary School's mothers' delegation, which had spearheaded the drive to oust the clerks, expressed satisfaction. "I think that's very white of those girls. They have our appreciation and thanks."

Barroom rowdies and racist groups had less to do with whipping up the anti-Japanese frenzy than public officials and journalists. Virulent, unabashed racism flowed freely from the mouths and pens of respected columnists, state representatives, U.S. senators, and army generals.

The press was particularly guilty of spreading rumor and speculation as fact. A story in the December 11 edition of the *Seattle Post-Intelligencer* (later proved false) was headlined: "Fifth Columnists Set Plane Beacon Fires Near Port Angeles." Syndicated columnist Henry McLemore, writing in the *San Francisco Examiner* and the *Seattle Times,* made his feelings clear: "Herd 'em up, pack 'em off and give them the inside room of the

Racist poster, 1942. Courtesy Vic Kubo.

badlands. Let 'em be pinched, hurt, hungry and dead up against it." Famed radio commentator Edward R. Murrow told an audience in Seattle in January 1942: "I think it's probable that, if Seattle ever does get bombed, you will be able to look up and see some University of Washing-

ton sweaters on the boys doing the bombing." Prominent journalists Walter Lippmann and John B. Hughes also joined the attack. The Japanese enemy was characterized in the media as degenerate, craven, and "rotten little devils."

Lieutenant General John DeWitt,

Rock of Ages

Takeo "Tom" Matsuoka picks up the rock he calls his "masterpiece" and holds it in the palm of his weathered hand. It's a polished, irregularly shaped stone, with a flat bottom and stratified colors—rust, purple, and dark green—like the bands of a planet.

More than 50 years ago, Matsuoka was among 129 Japanese from the Seattle area, leaders of the Japanese community, arrested by the FBI and incarcerated at federal detention centers in the weeks after Pearl Harbor.

"I never expected to be picked up and taken to camp," recalls Matsuoka. Though he was a Nisei, born in Hawaii, he could not find his birth certificate. The FBI was suspicious of his membership in the Japanese Association and his position as a leader of the Bellevue Vegetable Growers Association. He was arrested on December 8, 1941.

He was taken to Fort Missoula, Montana, along with other Japanese. Dozens of leaders of the Japanese community who had worked for decades to maintain family farms, run small businesses, and provide for their families suddenly found themselves with nothing to do.

Matsuoka doesn't remember exactly how it all started. It was in March 1942 when the snow was melting and the men began finding agate and soft stones from a field on the west side of the Rocky Mountains. Bringing the rocks back to their barracks, the men would rub them on the concrete floor of the shower room and shine them with their army blankets.

Soon everybody was shining rocks, which took the better part of a week, and displaying them in rock competitions in the mess hall. One of the internees wrote home to his wife about "rock fever."

"I guess she thought it was some kind of sickness," Matsuoka laughs. "She wrote back and told him she really hoped he would take care of that rock fever."

The rock-polishing craze slowly died down, and a few months later, Matsuoka was permitted to join family members in Tule Lake, California, at one of the 10 concentration camps run by the War Relocation Authority.

head of the Western Defense Command, left no doubt that Japanese and Japanese Americans were singled out for mass exclusion on racial grounds. In his final recommendation to Secretary of War Henry Stimson on the possibility of an evacuation, dated February 14, 1942, DeWitt wrote, "In the war in which we are now engaged racial affinities are not severed by migration. The Japanese race is an enemy race and while many second and third generation Japanese born on United States soil, possessed of United States citizenship, have become 'Americanized,' the racial strains are undiluted."

Claims that Japanese Americans should be removed because of potential sabotage (the "military necessity" argument) were patently false in view of reports to the contrary from the FBI, Office of Naval Intelligence, and Federal Communications Commission. The government also claimed Japanese Americans should be incarcerated "for their own protection," but as University of Michigan historian Gail Nomura observed, "In America, we lock up the criminal not the victim. Rather than imprisoning all Japanese Americans,...measures should have been taken to prevent any violence against Japanese Americans and prosecute any who committed acts of violence."

Another possible factor in the government's decision was the potential use of Issei or Nisei, even though they were U.S. citizens, as hostages in future prisoner exchanges with the Japanese. Author Michi Weglyn explores this theory at length in her seminal work *Years of Infamy,* presenting evidence that the Japanese mistreatment of American civilians in Japanese territory caused Stimson to call for "threats of reprisals" on Japanese nationals in the U.S.

On February 19, 1942, President Roosevelt signed Executive Order 9066. Although the order didn't mention Japanese Americans or resident aliens by name, it authorized the removal of "any or all persons" from designated military zones and transferred authority over civilians from the government to the military. The next day, Stimson appointed DeWitt military commander with orders to carry out the removal. In the ensuing weeks, the War Relocation Authority (WRA) was created to oversee the "evacuation." DeWitt then named Colonel Karl Bendetsen director of the Wartime Civil Control Administration (WCCA), which divided the West Coast into 108 exclusion zones.

Congress formed the Tolan Committee to investigate "national defense migration," but it proved to be no more than a rubber-stamp exercise. When the committee came to Washington state in early March, both Seattle Mayor Earl Millikin and

Governor Arthur Langlie declared their support of the removal.

"There is no doubt about those 8,000 Japanese, that 7,900 probably are above question," Millikin testified. "But the other 100 would burn this town down and let the Japanese planes come in and bring on something that would dwarf Pearl Harbor."

Said Langlie: "Every precaution should be made to be humane and American in this task, but the people feel this is not the time to worry about hurting feelings."

Washington state attorney general Smith Troy supplied two bizarre arguments for the exclusion, but no evidence: that mob violence against the Japanese was imminent and that enemy aliens posed a threat to the state's lumber industry. Japanese could hide out in forests and "raise havoc" by destroying the trees.

A noted opponent to the exclusion was Tacoma Mayor Harry Cain. The Methodist Preachers Association Committee of Seattle also sounded a note of reason in a statement: "These people are no more responsible for this war than we are. No acts of theirs now or in the past have given the slightest reason to impugn their good citizenship."

In mid-March a curfew was established from 8 P.M. to 6 A.M., hampering restaurants, men with night jobs, and university students. Yuri Takahashi, the 22-year-old manager

Posting of "evacuation" orders, April 1942. Courtesy Museum of History and Industry, Seattle Post-Intelligencer *Collection.*

tage of irrigation systems and valuable crops. Governors from a dozen western states opposed relocation to their states for similar reasons. About 500 Nikkei with family or friends outside the restricted zones packed up and moved east. At the University of Washington, the administration helped some of the several hundred Japanese American students, faculty, and staff transfer to eastern colleges.

By the end of March 1942, sites had been determined for "assembly centers," temporary prison camps, and more permanent "relocation centers." At the time, 14,400 Japanese and Japanese Americans lived in Washington state, 9,600 of them in King County. The Japanese population of Seattle was nearly 7,000.

Mrs. Fukuhara and daughter, Seiko, pack up their belongings in preparation for leaving Seattle, spring 1942. Courtesy Museum of History and Industry, Seattle Post-Intelligencer *Collection.*

EXPULSION

THE NEWS OF THEIR forced removal confirmed the worst fears of the Nisei, who had held out hope that any expulsion of Japanese would spare them as American citizens. Dwarfed by the enormity of the world at war, the injustice was unmistakably aimed at West Coast Japanese as an Asian ethnic group. The government never seriously considered rounding up Italian or German Americans en masse, though a number of immigrant

of the Sarashina Cafe in Seattle, told a newspaper reporter:

"It [the curfew] is a blow to us Nisei....Lots of restaurants down here will have to close hours early, but we must do as we are told." One young Nisei couple from South Park was so afraid to break the curfew that the pregnant wife didn't go to the hospital when she went into labor one night. The baby was born at home with the umbilical cord twisted around its neck and later died.

With the exclusion issue all but decided, the question arose as to where the Japanese would go. In Washington state, the restricted military zone covered the western third of the state. Officials in eastern Washington opposed resettlement there ostensibly because of possible sabo-

Evacuated Bainbridge Island Japanese Americans board the ferry, March 31, 1942. Courtesy Museum of History and Industry, Seattle Post-Intelligencer *Collection.*

"enemy aliens" were detained. Imagine the outcry from the American public if second-generation Italian American Joe DiMaggio, the beloved Yankee baseball star at the peak of his career, had been forced to leave his home and team for a desert concentration camp. Neither was there a mass expulsion of Japanese Americans from Hawaii, despite the fact they comprised 38 percent of the territory's population.

On March 30, 1942, Nikkei from Bainbridge Island in Puget Sound became the first group in the nation to be evacuated and incarcerated, presumably because of their proximity to the Puget Sound Navy Yard. They were given only one week to store or sell their belongings and find caretakers for their farms.

For decades, Japanese strawberry farmers had worked and lived alongside white farmers and neighbors. The sudden departure was wrenching for many island residents. At the ferry dock on March 30, the Japanese were seen off on a special 11:00 A.M. ferry by a large group of friends, many of them weeping—children

Higo 10 Cents Store on Jackson Street with boarded-up windows, April 1942. Courtesy Museum of History and Industry, Seattle Post-Intelligencer *Collection.*

who had cut school, baseball teammates, and housewives. As instructed, Nikkei brought only what they could carry. Some women clutched wildflowers and bits of greenery. When the boat arrived in Seattle, hundreds of curious bystanders jammed the Marion Street overpass to watch as the passengers were transferred to a train bound for imprisonment in Manzanar, California.

A few weeks later in Seattle, on Tuesday, April 21, "evacuation" announcements were posted on telephone poles and bulletin boards. The community was to leave the city in three groups the following Tuesday, Thursday, and Friday.

Although many felt an inner turmoil, a mingling of humiliation, anxiety, and resentment, the "evacuation" proceeded almost without incident, a fact that may be attributed to the Japanese stoic attitude toward adversity, *shikata ga nai,* "it cannot be helped." Nisei were also raised to respect authority, obey their elders, and not to stick out in a crowd. "They tell you one thing and then they tell you another, and a fellow doesn't know what he's going to do," said T. Hayashida, a Bainbridge Island strawberry farmer.

"But if this country thinks it is best for us to move, why, that's all right."

The local Japanese American Citizens League urged patriotism and cooperation in the extreme. In one proclamation, the JACL stated, "Whereas no sacrifice is too great in realizing our avowed objective in prosecuting this war to a successful conclusion; and whereas the government of the United States has taken extraordinary measures under the circumstances to safeguard the comfort, safety and economic welfare of the persons due to be evacuated; and whereas it is the first duty of the loyal American to obey the orders of their government; therefore be it resolved that the Japanese American Citizens League of Seattle go on record as indorsing [sic] cheerful and willful cooperation by the community with the government agencies in carrying out the evacuation proceedings...."

The JACL set up the Emergency Defense Council in a vacant store on Main Street to aid families of Issei taken away by the FBI and, eventually, to help people pack up and leave. Because the Army limited Nikkei to bringing only what they could carry, people made arrangements to store their belongings at churches or at the homes or businesses of friends. Sagamiya, the Japanese sweetshop in the heart of Nihonmachi, stored boxes and trunks piled to the ceiling. But many

Government official sorts through "contraband" radios, circa December 1942. Courtesy Museum of History and Industry, Seattle Post-Intelligencer Collection.

Whites Try to Buy Them Out at Low Price, Say Japanese

Seattle - born Japanese business men, facing possibilities of losing their establishments through evacuation, are doing business as usual here — but with their fingers crossed.

A few, however, already are conducting "removal sales," and many complain that they are being annoyed by white competitors, who want to buy the Japanese owner's stock at 5 or 10 cents on the dollar, now that the Japanese are faced with evacuation.

The Japanese know not at what time the government will order them to leave Seattle immediately. Neither do they know how long they will have to dispose of their stock.

Though Seattle's American-born Japanese are facing heavy losses,

they ask no sympathy. They say their greatest heartache is the severe blow to their pride in citizenship.

"Because we are good Americans and have been taught the American spirit, we can take it," said one. "We are anxious to do our part. It is a very small sacrifice for the right to be an American."

Presidents' Names Taken

A typical situation is that of the Beppu brothers, who operate a fishing-tackle store at 600 Third Ave. Named after Presidents, they are Taft, Lincoln and Grant Beppu. They have a younger brother, Monroe Beppu, who is in the United States Army. All were born in Seattle.

They have been in business eight years and were about to reap the profits of the approaching fishing season. Because of their business

Article, Seattle Times, *March 6, 1942.*

families were forced to sell nearly everything they owned for a fraction of its worth. Local newspapers were filled with "Evacuation Sale" ads for businesses and homes. One classified ad read: "Small South End restaurant for sale. Will Sacrifice. Tenant must evacuate."

Everyone with at least one-sixteenth Japanese blood had to leave. This included sisters Hazel and Grace Woo, whose mother was Nisei and whose father was Chinese American.

On the day of departure, Nikkei met at 8th Avenue South and South Lane Street and other departure points in the city, arriving with suitcases and duffel bags tagged with preassigned numbers. Among the friends who came to say goodbye was Ada Mahon, the longtime principal of Bailey Gatzert School, where 320 of the 720 students were Japanese Americans. Miss Mahon wept openly at the sight of her departing students.

A total of 12,892 persons of Japanese ancestry from Washington state were incarcerated. Seattle and Puyallup Valley Nikkei were sent to the Puyallup "assembly center" and then on to Minidoka in Idaho. Residents of rural King County, Kitsap County (except Bainbridge Island), Pierce County (except Puyallup Valley), and other western Washington counties were sent to another concentration camp at Tule Lake, California, via Pinedale, California. Those living in Yakima Valley and

Storefront of Japanese-run business, April 1942. Courtesy Museum of History and Industry, Seattle Post-Intelligencer Collection.

surrounding counties were eventually taken to Heart Mountain, Wyoming. Also incarcerated were 160 Nikkei from Alaska.

In the White River Valley, farmers bid tearful farewells to their homes and land. Shuji Kimura has vivid memories of the departure: "We didn't feel so bad about leaving with all the excitement of leaving. But soon when six p.m. came and the train began to move, and we saw Mr. Ballard waving his hat at us, his coat collar turned against the rain, mother began to cry. I couldn't see through my tears either. I saw the Main Street crossing, there were more people waving. The train began to go faster and the berry rows, the rhubarb fields, the lettuce fields and the pea fields began to slip past our window like a panorama. My throat hurt, but I couldn't take my

eyes from the familiar fields and pastures slipping so quickly away."

An estimated 600 to 900 farms were abandoned in King County, most of them taken over by whites and Filipinos.

The massive scale of the injustice was almost beyond comprehension for most of the prisoners, but it wasn't without precedent. In the 1830s, the U.S. government moved Choctaws, Cherokees, Chickasaws, and Creeks from their homelands in Georgia, Alabama, and Mississippi to reservations west of the Mississippi River under the Indian Removal Bill of 1830.

It bears repeating that none of the Japanese American prisoners was accused or convicted of any crime. None had been advised of his civil or constitutional rights or given the right to legal counsel. None was ever charged with or convicted of espionage or sabotage before, during, or after the war. One hundred and ten thousand people were presumed guilty and deprived of their freedom for up to three years.

Issei Katsuko Hirata was moved to write:

To endless heartache and pain
we resign ourselves
to our fate, again and again.

Is this the peaceful life?
Getting in the way and hated
just for living.

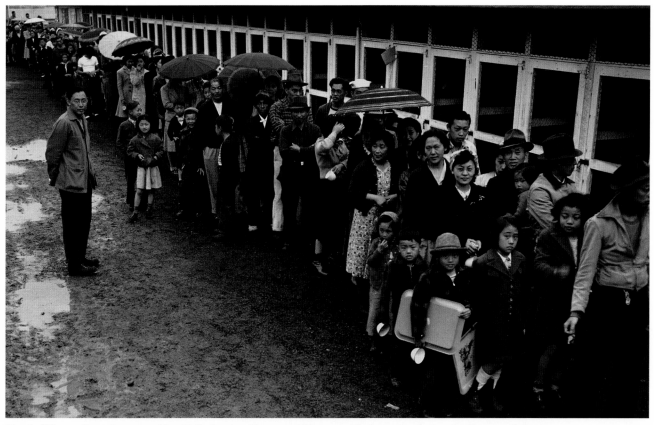

Mess hall line at Camp Harmony, May 1942. Courtesy Museum of History and Industry, Seattle Post-Intelligencer *Collection.*

CAMP HARMONY

NIKKEI RODE IN vans, buses, and private automobiles about 25 miles south of Seattle to the Puyallup Assembly Center on the site of the annual Western Washington State Fair, where they remained from April 28 to September 23, 1942.

If they held out hope for a mea-sure of freedom—the belief they were simply being "relocated," not detained—there remained little doubt of their imprisonment upon their arrival at "Camp Harmony," a make-shift city constructed in 17 days under the jurisdiction of the Wartime Civil Control Administration (WCCA).

"Mike," a young friend of author Anne Reeploeg Fisher's, wrote her of his first impressions: "As the rows and rows of shacks loomed up be-fore me as the bus turned the bend, I felt myself overcome with a feeling of depression. I saw the nine-foot fences surrounded with a wave of barbed wire. I saw soldiers with [guns] patrolling each and every side....And then the gates shut be-hind me. It seemed as if I had been 'sent up the river' and I had a feeling I wanted to go home."

Against a surreal backdrop of a racetrack, roller coaster, and Ferris

The First Day

Like most young women of the day, Tama Tokuda (née Inouye) had led a sheltered life and, at the age of 21, felt more teenager than adult. After Japan bombed Pearl Harbor and the "evacuation" loomed, her feelings of uncertainty and vulnerability intensified. Beginning in the spring of 1942, Tama kept a diary, recording her impressions of the tumultuous events of the era. The following entry describes the day she and her family left Seattle and were taken to the "assembly center" in Puyallup.

Toshiko B., Toshiko H., and Ruth Haines came to see me off....I felt terribly low and lost and haggard as the bus started to move. It was so quiet during the ride but I noticed a tear rolling down my mother's face.

When we arrived at the gates of Camp Harmony on the Puyallup Fairgrounds, I noticed the fence with the barbed wires. There were soldiers and a guard tower with a manned machine gun. We were the enemy. Quietly we left the bus and were directed to our apartment which turned out to be a bare room with a light bulb hanging down in the center of the room. Tufts of grass stuck out between the floor boards and the partition of the side wall did not go completely to the ceiling.

Papa said that we were to go to a certain room to get our mattresses so I followed him. There were some young men in the room with hay piled in the corner. They helped us stuff some mattresses and carried them back to our place. We 4 kids were given wooden cots and our parents were given steel ones that were supposed to be more comfortable.

On our first night in this strange world, someone knocked on our door at 10 PM. "Lights out," he said. We were already in bed as we had been forewarned about the curfew. Soon there was a circle of light that lit the ceiling. There were some bachelors in the next room and one of them had lit a cigarette. Very shortly, we heard the crackling of paper and then someone crunching. My sister and I could tell that one of the men had had the foresight to bring potato chips. After a somber exhausting day, the sound triggered a funny bone. We started to giggle and couldn't stop for a long time.

wheel, barracks had been constructed in converted livestock stalls, under grandstands, and on parking lots. The camp was divided into four areas lettered A through D, complete with "apartments," mess halls, and other facilities. Movement between areas was restricted except by special pass.

Boards were laid flat on the ground for floors and grass grew between the cracks. Some mattresses were issued, but most inmates had to stuff straw into canvas bags. Rooms were equipped with woodstoves, army cots, and blankets. The Nikkei made chairs and tables out of boxes and scrap lumber. Frequent complaints were registered about leaking roofs, the lack of hot water, and the scarcity of food items. Inmates wore Japanese *geta* to negotiate the ubiquitous mud on the way to mess halls, latrines, and laundry rooms. By summer, the population of the camp swelled to more than 7,500, including 1,200 people from the Puyallup Valley area and a small number from Alaska.

The lack of privacy was perhaps the most degrading aspect of camp life. Old and young alike shared shower and toilet facilities. The "toilets" consisted of wooden planks with six holes cut into each board. Family "apartments" were rooms, measuring 8 by 10 feet or 15 by 20 feet, separated by walls that didn't reach all the way to the ceiling.

The Yoshimura family unpacks in their room at Camp Harmony. From left: Irwin, Ruth, Bruce and Denny Yoshimura; Frances and Yuki Harada. Courtesy Museum of History and Industry, Seattle Post-Intelligencer *Collection.*

Camp Harmony latrine, painting by Hisashi Hagiya, 1942. Courtesy Wing Luke Asian Museum, Jack Kudo Collection.

Children could look through knot-holes and cracks in wall boards to the adjoining room. Nikkei remember hearing noise from crying babies and lovemaking while they tried to sleep.

Camp Harmony residents were treated as prisoners and denied basic constitutional rights: the right to assemble except by permission of authorities, religious freedom (Shinto was banned), free speech (most Japanese-language books were confiscated), and privacy (police didn't need warrants to search living quarters). The inmates also endured a host of petty regulations such as roll call, curfew, set mealtimes, and lights-out. When circumstances warranted exceptions, camp procedures called for written requests that could be as humiliating as they were ridiculous. Wrote one young father to the authorities, "I hereby submit my application for permission to turn on a shaded light between the hours of 10:30 p.m. and 6:00 a.m., if necessary for the proper care of a child aged 20+ months. Lights will be turned on for short intervals only, and only for the purpose of changing diapers or calming the child if necessary. Thank you for your consideration."

Historical accounts of the incarceration tend to stress the massive scale of the experience, the "herding" of people, the "mass evacuation," but the events of 1942 were

Children play Monopoly in Camp Harmony, circa May 1942. Courtesy Museum of History and Industry, Seattle Post-Intelligencer *Collection.*

experienced in tens of thousands of individual lives and minds. The prisoners at Camp Harmony were as diverse as any other population of several thousand people: people of all ages, education, and professions. Disabled people, pregnant mothers, doctors, lawyers, laborers, students. Bullies, victims, optimists, pessimists. Sports heroes, dancers, musicians. Sick people, abandoned orphans.

The inmates tried to impose the appearance of normal life on the drab Puyallup center. A local government was formed under the aegis of the JACL, which had worked with the WCCA on the details of the evacuation. Inmates worked at various jobs around camp for wages of under $20 per month. They published a newsletter. For the sake of familiarity, mess halls were named after popular Seattle restaurants—Jackson Cafe, Spike Cafe, Blanc's Cafe—and dished up army-type food: Vienna sausages, potatoes, and vegetables. On weekends, white friends of Japanese Americans visited, along with curious strangers who came to gawk at the inmates through the barbed wire as if they were animals in a zoo.

Young people played among the grandstands and rides and in sports competitions of volleyball, baseball, and *sumo*. In the evenings, they danced to music from portable radios set to the same station and a big band called the Harmonaires. Special graduation ceremonies were held in June for evacuated high school seniors.

Some of the Nisei, especially those in the JACL, continued to preach cooperation above all else. The JACL position went beyond acquiescence, actively opposing any dissent. In the months after Pearl Harbor, Clarence Arai headed a JACL committee to report subversive activities in the Japanese community to the FBI. In a bulletin to JACL chapters in April 1942, Mike Masaoka of the national JACL urged nonsupport of Minoru Yasui, a Nisei lawyer who had recently been convicted of violating the curfew in Portland. Later, the JACL refused to back draft resisters in the inland concentration camps.

The JACL line was by no means representative of the community as a whole. Far from the stereotype of the docile "quiet Americans" portrayed in some postwar histories, Nikkei held widely divergent and vociferous viewpoints. A number of Issei and Kibei bitterly resented the JACL Nisei for apparently collaborating with government officials to facilitate the incarceration and iden-tify Issei leaders for the FBI. The division was especially heated at the concentration camp in Manzanar, California, where prisoners rioted in December 1942. JACL leaders in Camp Harmony also feared for their lives. Seattle Nisei attorneys Thomas Shinao Masuda and Kenji Ito openly challenged the JACL's authority, con-tending that the Nisei administra-tion was undemocratic, because its leaders were not elected, and that the JACL was a tool of the U.S. government. Although the JACL re-ceived a vote of confidence in a campwide election, by the time the community was relocated to Minidoka, the tide of opinion had turned on James Sakamoto and other JACL leaders. As a result, they had little say in how Minidoka was run.

However misguided and self-serving, the JACL fervently believed it was acting in the community's best interest. With Issei community leaders interned in Justice Depart-ment camps throughout the coun-try, the burden of community lead-ership had fallen by default on the Nisei, who were young—about 19 years old on average—and inexpe-rienced. Japanese Americans were in a poor position to fight the expul-sion. Years of segregation and dis-enfranchisement had left the com-munity with no real voice in local or national politics. JACL leaders were advised by the military authorities not to resist.

Crowds gather at Camp Harmony to say goodbye to friends who are headed for imprisonment at the Minidoka concentration camp, August 1942. Courtesy Museum of History and Industry, Seattle Post-Intelligencer *Collection.*

Mud at the Minidoka concentration camp, November 1943. War Relocation Authority photo published in the Seattle Times.

"Today, Sansei [third generation] and Yonsei [fourth generation] blame the second generation for evacuating quietly, doing what the Army said, but they had reason to do so," says Misao Sakamoto, widow of James Sakamoto. "I guess we were all scared so we just went. Of course we were told that if we didn't go they would move us at the point of a gun anyway. There wasn't any choice."

"We don't blame the Nisei," insists Frank Abe, a Seattle redress activist and journalist. "There's a difference between blaming and holding the leadership responsible for its actions."

Japanese American inmates farm land adjacent to Minidoka camp, circa 1943. Courtesy Maeda Family Collection.

ON TO MINIDOKA

BEGINNING ON AUGUST 10, 1942, most Nikkei from Seattle were sent to the "Minidoka Relocation Center" near Hunt, Idaho, about 15 miles from Twin Falls and 150 miles southeast of Boise. The town of Minidoka actually lay several miles to the east. The camp got its name because the land—68,000 acres in all—was part of a massive government irrigation effort known as the Minidoka Reclamation Project.

During the 27-hour train ride from Puyallup, the prisoners were ordered to keep the blinds shut. If they had been able to look outside, they would have seen a remarkable transformation of terrain from the lush forests on the west side of the Cascade Mountains, along the Columbia River, over flatlands and rolling hills, and finally to the 4,000-foot elevation of the southern Idaho prairie. As they stepped off the train in Eden, the only color in the drab landscape was the wan blue sky and the ever-present sagebrush, the color of green mold. They boarded a rickety army bus to the camp, which they soon discovered was only partially completed.

"We were disgusted enough just looking at the place, scorching under a 110-degree sun, so you can imagine how we felt when we were told that our rooms were not yet

Boys eat wieners in the Minidoka camp mess hall, circa 1943. Courtesy Wing Luke Asian Museum, Hatate Family Collection.

Children march in parade near Minidoka barracks, circa 1943. Courtesy Wing Luke Asian Museum, Hatate Family Collection.

"Kimi-chan"

May Sasaki was six years old at the start of the war and spent three impressionable years in confinement at the Minidoka camp in southern Idaho. Most of the time, she felt like any other American youngster, going to school and playing with her friends. But even at that young age, she sensed the import of the incarceration.

Fifty-plus years later, her memories are tempered with an adult awareness of how the experience affected her nascent self-identity. Her views were recorded on videotape for the Densho Project, a Seattle-based organization that is compiling a digital archive of personal visual histories and historic photographs.

[My teacher in camp tried] to make us feel that the situation was very unfortunate, but [I] don't feel that we were guilty of anything. Although I did feel guilty because we were in—even at that age I could understand that we were behind this [fence]—and then the watch guards were always [there]....

Well, it must have left something because up until the time I had gone into camp, everyone referred to me with my Japanese name, which was Kimiko. So I was always "Kimi-chan," and that was okay. But I began to sense that it was because I was Japanese that I was in this camp because I looked around and we were all Japanese.

And I think that's when I came to this decision that whenever I get out of here, I'm not gonna be Japanese anymore. At that age, it doesn't make any sense but that's what I decided. I never said anything to anyone, but I remember that near the end when we were ready to leave, when people would call me "Kimi-chan," I would pretend not to hear them. I could hear them muttering and everything, but I wouldn't hear them, and I figured that's the way I'm going to do it. I'm not going to be Kimiko anymore. I'm going to be May because that's my name also.

And I never used my name Kimiko after.

completed," "Mike" wrote in a letter to Anne Reeploeg Fisher. "Some people just broke down and bawled....There are many rattlesnakes and scorpions and besides these there are black widows, bull snakes, beetles, horned toads and of course the very persistent mosquito—we're all just one happy family."

Once inside the camp, the inmates stood in line in the blazing heat for a medical examination before being taken to their living quarters.

For the first few weeks, there was no hot water, and often no water at all, as construction workers shut off mains to complete their work. Camp residents watched in dismay as builders erected the final barriers to freedom: a barbed wire fence—which was electrified at first—and guard towers, manned by armed soldiers. Although there were no shooting

Issei women wash dishes in Minidoka mess hall, circa 1943. Norio Mitsuoka photo.

deaths at Minidoka, there were incidents at other camps.

The 7,050 Nikkei from the Seattle area were joined by 2,500 from Oregon and 150 from Alaska—some of them children or grandchildren of Eskimo women and Japanese men.

The 500 barracks were arranged in 44 blocks, each block with two sections of six barracks, served by a mess hall and a central H-shaped shower and toilet facility with no privacy. Family rooms varied depending on family size, averaging 16 by 20 feet, and were equipped only with a potbellied stove and canvas army cots. The entire residence area was two and a half miles long and a mile wide, roughly equivalent in length to the area in downtown Seattle from the base of Queen Anne Hill to South Dearborn and in width from the waterfront to Seattle University. Seattle was evacuated by neighborhood, so neighbors were mostly housed together in the same block and elected their own block managers. Other buildings in the camp included a hospital, administration buildings, staff apartments, a warehouse, churches, and schools.

In late summer 1942, 2,000 Japanese American inmates helped harvest the local sugar beet, onion, and potato crops, alleviating a severe manpower shortage. As temperatures dipped, camp residents, faced with a lack of coal, gathered sagebrush to burn in their stoves. Severe weather was one of the chief hardships for people who had lived all their lives in the temperate climate of western Washington and Oregon. Winters were harshly cold, often 10 to 20 degrees below zero, and the thin walls of the barracks provided the barest protection against icy winds. In the summer, temperatures climbed as high as 115 degrees. After it rained, the dust became a thick bog of mud.

Like many Nikkei, Yukiko Miyake's dominant memory is of the swirling brown dust, actually powdery ash from a prehistoric volcanic eruption. "The sand storms came once every two to three months and lasted about half an hour," she recalls. "The first time I was in one, I'd just washed my hair and was going to visit someone. I got [to my friend's] and had to wash my hair again. My scarf and hair were thick with sand. Sand would get into the house and everywhere."

The inmates coped as best they could with the indignity of shared

The Yamaguchi family in their living quarters at Minidoka, circa 1943. Courtesy Wing Luke Asian Museum, Hatate Family Collection.

Two girls in the high school at Minidoka, circa 1943. Courtesy Wing Luke Asian Museum, Hatate Family Collection.

Swimmers cool off in the canal at the edge of the Minidoka camp. Courtesy Wing Luke Asian Museum, Hatate Family Collection.

housing and bathing facilities—including, in the first months, open-pit latrines—and the lingering anger and shame of their eviction from lifelong homes and neighborhoods. Minidoka became a little American city. Residents formed community groups, churches of many denominations, schools, newspapers, and craft classes. They opened a library with donated books and staffed a camp fire station and hospital. Young people joined Boy Scout and Girl Scout troops, bands, and sports teams. The "Sagebrush World Series" pitted teams from Blocks 1 through 19 against 20 to 44. Nearly every week, there were dances at the mess halls and movies at the recreation center. The Minidoka Mass Choir, permitted to leave camp and perform in neighboring towns, was considered one of the best choirs in southern Idaho. Residents even staged their own beauty contest, the "Sweetheart of Minidoka," with contestants representing each block.

Half the inmates worked for wages similar to those paid at Camp Harmony: from $12 per month for clerical work to $19 a month for professional work. Japanese American doctors made this top wage working at the camp hospital alongside Caucasian doctors earning many times more a month. At the cafeteria-style mess halls, Issei women helped in the kitchen, served food, and washed dishes.

Social life continued under unusual conditions. This item appeared in the camp newspaper, the *Minidoka Irrigator:*

"Reminding post-midnight romancers that social rooms are provided for dates, the Internal Security Division this week warned couples to stay out of laundry rooms and shower rooms. If any more are found, names will be taken down, and some drastic action taken, it was said."

As in any prison-like setting, passing idle time became a major challenge. Issei men played *go* and *shogi* (Japanese chess). Gardeners created order and beauty out of desert shrubs, wildflowers, sand, and rocks. One popular avocation was wood carving. Yoichi Matsuda remembers crawling under the barbed wire fence to gather greasewood, a gnarled woody shrub, later to carve it into lacquered pins, lampstands, and sculptures. Carpenters fashioned furniture out of stolen scrap wood. One of these woodworkers was Seattle native George Nakashima, who went on to become a world-renowned furniture designer.

Another famed Minidokan was the brilliant artist Kenjiro Nomura, whose paintings had been exhibited at the Museum of Modern Art in New York in the 1930s. As he had in Nihonmachi in Seattle, Nomura worked as a sign painter for restrooms, mess halls, and canteens.

Lillian Suzuki carries pails of water between barracks at Minidoka, circa 1943. Emery Andrews photo, courtesy Bill Kunitsugu.

Public ceremony near the flagpole in Minidoka, March 1943. Seattle Times *photo.*

During the holidays, Minidokans made do with homemade toys and gifts donated by churches from Seattle. A Nisei bard captured the flavor of the first Christmas in confinement:

The Idaho rain had come down
*   in a flush,*
The sprinkling of snow was
*   turning to slush.*

When what to my wondering eyes
*   should appear,*
But a miniature sleigh and eight
*   tiny reindeer*

With a little old driver so lively
*   and quick*
With a retreaded sack and
*   boots synthetic*

From head to toe the picture
*   of yule*
With his big red suit of reprocessed
*   wool.*

He jumped from his sleigh with a
*   "Hiya Bud"*
And promptly sank in the
*   Hunt City Mud.*

As the months and years passed, Minidoka took on the look of a more permanent settlement. The tar paper on the barracks became weathered and puckered. Saplings grew into small trees. Stones lined walkways. On the northern edge of camp, inmates dug a seven-mile irrigation ditch and farmed 1,000 acres of vegetables. Many grew accustomed to the desert landscape. Wrote Monica Sone: "This was a strange, gaunt country, fierce in the hot white light of day, but soft and gentle with a beauty all its own at night." Indoors, rooms were filled with furniture and clothing bought from Sears catalogs or at stores in nearby Twin Falls, where Nikkei could visit on one-day passes.

Although the government insisted the camps were "relocation centers" and not prisons or "internment camps," the restrictions amounted to imprisonment. Besides the obvious fences, armed sentries, and guard towers, there were numerous infringements of civil rights. Private enterprise was forbidden, though Japanese food and other services were sold on the sly.

A few non-Japanese from Seattle stayed in touch with their Nikkei friends. The Reverend Emery E. Andrews of the Japanese Baptist Church followed his mostly Japanese American congregation to Idaho, renting a house in nearby Twin Falls. "Our whole family was brought up in the Japanese community and all their friends were there," said Andrews in an interview years later with the *Seattle Post-Intelligencer.* "My daughters actually cried because they couldn't go behind the barbed wire and live with their friends."

Andrews made 56 round-trips back to Seattle to pick up and deliver documents, messages, and pieces of furniture. Seattle Quaker activist Floyd Schmoe also made frequent visits to Minidoka, ferrying messages and supplies back and forth, particularly as relocation programs got under way.

"Our whole family was brought up in the Japanese community and all their friends were there....My daughters actually cried because they couldn't go behind the barbed wire and live with their friends."

Camp experience varied widely with the age and background of the inmates. Children generally enjoyed the freedom and endless possibilities for play. Composer Paul Chihara is almost embarrassed by the admission that his musical career was launched at Minidoka. As a boy of four, he was asked to get up and sing songs at the mess hall. Chihara's memories of camp are less of turbulent emotion than the normal pleasures of childhood. "Now that I'm older, I understand what my parents

went through and also my older siblings," he said. "But at my age and station in life, the whole experience hit me quite differently. I remember coming back to Seattle and asking my mother when we were going back to camp."

Most Nikkei "made the best of a bad situation." Former Minidokans have fond memories of meeting many new friends and future spouses. Some older Issei had a chance to relax for the first time in their adult lives, free of the responsibility of making a living and even of cooking dinner. Women, too, felt liberated by changes in expectations and day-to-day duties. When Nisei men went off to war, the women took their places as fire wardens and block managers, and filled other positions.

The "bad situation," however, had its costs. Besides utter boredom, some inmates suffered from severe depression and other mental illnesses due to their confinement or separation from family members. One mother, in the depths of such a depression, killed her baby with a hammer. Some older Minidokans suffered from chronic constipation because they were afraid to use the unpartitioned toilets. Campwide epidemics of diarrhea were not uncommon from the poor diet.

Many family relationships deteriorated. Parents found it difficult to keep families together now that meals were eaten in large mess halls; children often ate with their friends. Most young people were well behaved, but a number of them, no longer financially dependent on or beholden to their Issei parents, became more defiant of authority. In 1945, a few students broke into the Hunt High School building, destroying property, supplies, and files.

Older children seemed to experience the most confusion. One Nisei wrote a family friend in Seattle about his family's fate: "I just can't see why the government must coop us up after throwing us in the middle of the sage country with nothing but sagebrush for miles around. If this is democracy, I think I'd rather be under a stern dictatorship. At least I wouldn't be winding up behind barbed wire fences every time!"

Schools provided a good measure of normalcy—in elementary school, children began their day with the pledge of allegiance to the American flag—but some older students were frustrated by the uncertainty of life after camp. Wrote a 10th grade girl at Minidoka: "My life's ambition was to be a nurse and though I think of it often, yet, I'm afraid, very much afraid that I will be unable to carry out my plans....I have lost interest in school and in leaving; my desire for a nursing career has lessened; and I am a pessimist."

In general, Issei suffered from a profound diminution of authority and community stature. These proud, hardworking men and women had to rely increasingly on their children for translations of various instructions and rules and for leadership in community affairs.

As in any other city of 9,700, life and death went on in the form of weddings, births, religious confirmations, graduations, and funerals.

THE QUESTION OF LOYALTY

IN JANUARY 1943, the headline in the *Irrigator* screamed: "ARMY WILL ADMIT NISEI."

President Roosevelt's blessing of the War Department plan to create a segregated Nisei unit revealed either galling ignorance or hypocrisy: "No loyal citizen of the United States should be denied the democratic right to exercise the responsibilities of his citizenship, regardless of his ancestry. The principle on which this country was founded and by which it has always been governed is that Americanism is a matter of mind and heart; Americanism is not, and never was, a matter of race or ancestry...."

Many young men were eager to volunteer in the hope of improving the postwar status of their families. Other Nisei and their families ago-nized over the possibility of military service. While white American soldiers could go to war assured that their loved ones would be safe, Nisei still worried about the eventual fate of their families. Would they ever be able to return to their homes? Would there be prolonged detainment? Would they be forcibly sent to Japan?

Emotions reached a fever pitch on both sides of the issue. After Issei camp leader Yoshito Fujii accompanied government recruiters around Minidoka, someone erected a Japanese grave marker with his name on it on a nearby hill.

The tensions heightened with the issuance of two government questionnaires in February 1943. One was designed to determine the loyalty of potential volunteers and draftees. A second questionnaire, called an "Application for Leave Clearance," posed similar questions to all adults as a way to screen those who wished to leave camp under a government relocation program. Both forms contained two questions regarding the loyalty of the inmates: "Are you willing to serve in the armed forces of the United States on combat duty, wherever ordered?" (No. 27) and "Will you swear unqualified allegiance to the United States of America and faithfully defend the United States from any and all attacks by foreign or domestic forces and forswear any form of allegiance or obedience to the Japanese Emperor, or any other foreign government, power, or organization?" (No. 28).

Extensive public discussion helped Minidoka officials avoid the turmoil that took place at other concentration camps, but even at Minidoka, the questions created divisions within families and the community that remain even to this day.

Question 27 triggered deep resentment among some Nisei. After being stripped of their civil rights as American citizens, male inmates were being asked to shed blood in defense of these rights.

Many Nisei regarded question 28 as a trick question on the order of "Have you stopped beating your wife?" A "yes" answer would imply they had some allegiance to Japan to forswear; a "no" answer would be interpreted as disloyalty. The question posed an impossible dilemma

for the Issei: a "yes" would render them stateless, since U.S. law did not allow them to become naturalized U.S. citizens. The question was later changed for Issei to read: "Will you swear to abide by the laws of the United States and to take no action which would in any way interfere with the war effort of the United States?"

Of the 78,000 people throughout the 10 camps who were required to fill out the questionnaire, 75,000 filled them out and 6,700 answered "no" to question 28.

There were various reasons for replying "no." In some cases Issei parents begged their children to answer "no," fearing their families would be permanently separated. Some of those filling out the Application for Leave Clearance answered "no" because they didn't want to leave camp and face antagonism and possible violence in the outside

While white American soldiers could go to war assured that their loved ones would be safe, Nisei still worried about the eventual fate of their families.

27. Are you willing to serve in the armed forces of the United States on combat duty, wherever ordered? _____

28. Will you swear unqualified allegiance to the United States of America and faithfully defend the United States from any or all attack by foreign or domestic forces, and forswear any form of allegiance or obedience to the Japanese emperor, or any other foreign government, power, or organization? _____

_____
(Date)

_____
(Signature)

NOTE.—Any person who knowingly and wilfully falsifies or conceals a material fact or makes a false or fraudulent statement or representation in any matter within the jurisdiction of any department or agency of the United States is liable to a fine of not more than $10,000 or 10 years' imprisonment, or both.

U. S. GOVERNMENT PRINTING OFFICE   16—32565-1

Government-issued questionnaire, February 1943.

world. Others thought it an act of conscience and protest against the injustice of their imprisonment. A few were so embittered by their incarceration that they answered "no" and chose to renounce their American citizenship and go to Japan. Clearly, individuals' answers did not necessarily reflect their loyalty to the U.S.

A number of Nisei registered their outrage by replying "no" to both questions and acquired the pejorative nickname "no-no boys." Most of these protesters were segregated as "disloyals" and sent to a special "segregation center" at the Tule Lake concentration camp in northeast California, which had the greatest number of "no-nos." More than 250 so-called disloyals from Minidoka were sent to Tule Lake.

Another crisis erupted when the government reinstated the draft for Nisei in January 1944, and 63 draft resisters at Heart Mountain and some at other concentration camps took a principled stand to refuse induction until their constitutional rights were restored. Most Nisei of draft age had been reclassified in December 1941 to IV-F, a category of men ineligible for service because of physical, mental, or moral defect, and then, in September 1942, to IV-C, or enemy alien.

Jim Akutsu was one resister at Minidoka. Akutsu attempted to join the army in late December 1941 but was declared ineligible and was later reclassified as IV-C. In camp, Akutsu answered "no" to question 28, believing a "yes" reply would incriminate him as once having loyalty to the Japanese emperor. Upon resisting the draft in 1944, he was arrested and sent to McNeil Island Penitentiary for nearly four years until he and other Nisei resisters received a pardon from President Truman in 1947.

"If the U.S. Constitution and Bill of Rights didn't apply to me by putting me in camp and classifying me as IV-C, enemy alien, then why should the Selective Service laws apply?" Akutsu says of his wartime decision. "I was *made* an alien by the United States government."

Akutsu applied for repatriation to Japan but was never sent.

Seattle author John Okada based much of his classic novel *No-No Boy* on Akutsu's experiences. Ichiro Yamada, the book's main character, speaks passionately of his refusal to serve in the military: "You can't make me go in the Army because I'm not an American or you wouldn't have plucked me and mine from a life that was good and real and meaningful and fenced me in the desert like they do the Jews in Germany and it is a puzzle why you haven't started to liquidate us though you might as well since everything else has been destroyed."

DISTINGUISHED MILITARY SERVICE

A SIGNIFICANT NUMBER of Nisei men decided they had only one alternative: to prove their loyalty and citizenship by joining the army (Nisei were officially barred from other branches of military service). Declared one Nisei at Minidoka: "If we are to clinch the case for ourselves, once and for all, and if we are to be embodied in the American grain so conclusively that we can never again be smeared and reviled by the bigots and the home fascists, there is no course for the eligible among us but to try like hell to get into the uniforms of Uncle Sam's fighting forces." More than 300 men from Minidoka volunteered for the newly formed all-Nisei battalion, the highest number from any concentration camp.

Often against the wishes of anguished parents, a total of more than 33,000 Japanese American men and women (in the Women's Army Corps) served in World War II. The 100th Infantry Battalion, made up of volunteers and draftees from Hawaii and the mainland, was absorbed by the 442nd Regimental Combat Team, and their motto was "Go for Broke!" a Hawaiian pidgin phrase meaning "go all the way."

The 100th/442nd fought in Italy, France, and central Europe in seven major campaigns from 1943 to 1945. In battle after battle, Nisei soldiers showed bravery and fortitude under fire, sometimes sacrificing their own lives to protect others. "These are some of the best goddamn fighters in the U.S. Army," marveled Lieutenant General Mark W. Clark, commanding officer of the 5th Army. "If you have more, send them over."

Perhaps the most celebrated battle was the rescue of the "Lost Battalion," a group of Texas soldiers surrounded by German troops in the Vosges Mountains of northeastern France. It was October 1944. Nisei veterans of the battle recall "falling asleep in trenches half filled with water," and the incessant barrage of German artillery shells as they made their final assault. In six days of furious action, the 442nd suffered 814 casualties, including 140 deaths, in rescuing 211 men.

Another unit of the 442nd, the 522nd Field Artillery Battalion, participated in the liberation of the Nazi death camp at Dachau as part of the 7th Army's attack on Germany. This story has only recently come to light because soldiers in the 522nd were under army orders never to reveal their role in the liberation.

For its size and length of service, the 100th/442nd was the most highly decorated unit in the entire war, receiving seven Presidential Unit Citations, more than 18,000 individual decorations, and one Congressional Medal of Honor. It also suffered an enormously high number of casualties: 9,486 with 680 killed in action. Of all the concentration camps, Minidoka suffered the greatest number of injured and dead.

Less glorified, but equally important to the outcome of the war, were the more than 6,000 Japanese Americans who served in the Army Military Intelligence Service (MIS). Stationed with every major military unit in the Pacific, MIS soldiers broke Japanese radio codes, translated captured documents, and served as interpreters in the interrogation of prisoners.

Hank Gosho, son of a Seattle pharmacist, was nicknamed "Horizontal Hank" because he was pinned down so often by machine-gun fire. He saved a platoon of "Merrill's Marauders" by translating the machine gunners' orders. One non-Nisei member of the platoon wrote a letter home to his family: "Now we know and the Marauders want you to know that they are backing the Nisei 100 percent. It makes the boys and myself raging mad to read about movements against Japanese Americans by the 4-Fers back home. We should dare them to say things like they have in front of us."

General Charles Willoughby quantified his accolades: "The Nisei saved a million lives and shortened the war by two years."

The estimated 4,000 Nisei military

100th Infantry Battalion soldiers receive awards from Lieutenant General Mark Clark, 1944. U.S. Army photo.

Soldiers patrol the bombed-out streets of Livorno (Leghorn), Italy, July 19, 1944. U.S. Army photo, courtesy Nisei Veterans Committee.

volunteers inducted before the start of the war had been given menial, noncombat roles after the Japanese bombed Pearl Harbor. Others were discharged. A number of the men who had already enlisted formally protested when in 1944 the government reassigned them to combat roles. Some who caused problems or showed their "disloyalty" by answering "no" to question 28 on the loyalty questionnaire were demoted to a labor battalion made up of "suspect" U.S. soldiers of Japanese, German, and Italian descent.

Memorial service in Minidoka for Nisei soldiers killed in action, 1944. Courtesy Seiichi Hara Collection.

Eventually known as the 1800 Engineer General Service Battalion, the unit moved equipment and repaired bridges and roads in Tennessee, Mississippi, Louisiana, and Arkansas.

At Minidoka and the other camps, ceremonies for soldiers killed in combat became distressingly more common. Like thousands of other parents of fallen American soldiers, the Issei mourned the loss of their sons. Parents received American flags from military authorities, flags that had covered coffins at funerals they were unable to attend. The names of the young men began to add up and resonate: Pete Fujino, Francis Kinoshita, Tadao Sato, Yukio Sato, George Tatsumi, Setsuro Yamashita....

COURT CHALLENGES, CONTINUED HOSTILITY

OUTSIDE THE CAMPS, the expulsion of Japanese Americans from the West Coast was being challenged for the first time in court. Only a handful of Nikkei had resisted the curfew and removal orders, and most of their cases reached the Supreme Court. Californian Fred Korematsu changed his name and altered his appearance to avoid imprisonment and remain with his Caucasian girlfriend. Attorney Minoru Yasui of Portland,

The War Dead

★ ★ ★ ★ ★

Fifty-six Japanese American soldiers from Washington state died fighting for their country during the Second World War. Most were killed in action in Italy or France in the last year of the war. At the time of their deaths, they ranged in age from 19 to 37.

Eugene Takasuke (Beefo) Amabe
Robert Endo
Yasuo (Pete) Fujino
Peter Fujiwara
Edwin Yukio Fukui
Eiichi Fred Haita
Tom S. Haji
Ben Kayji Hara
John Hashimoto
Eugene Hayashi
Masao (Horse) Ikeda
William Imamoto
Shunichi Bill Imoto
Masami Inatsu
Mitsuo M. (Mike) Iseri
Haruo Suyama Ishida
Hisashi Iwai
Joe Yazuru Kadoyama
John Kanazawa
Jero Kanetomi
Akira Kanzaki
Yoshio Kato
John Ryoji Kawaguchi
Francis T. (Bako) Kinoshita
Isamu Kunimatsu
George M. Mayeda
William Shinji Mizukami
Masaki Nakamura

Ned Teiji Nakamura
William Kenzo Nakamura
Ban Ninomiya
Yoshito Noritake
Isao Okazaki
Takaaki Okazaki
Ken Omura
Satoru Onodera
Yohei Sagami
Tadao Sato
Yukio Sato
George Katsuya Sawada
Toll Seike
Tetsuo Shigaya
Frank Masao Shigemura
Jimmie Toshio Shimizu
Manzo (Mon) Takahashi
Jim Takeda
Shoichi Takehara
William Hiroshi Taketa
Masaru Richard Tamura
Matsusaburo Matt Tanaka
George Tatsumi
Theodore H. Watanabe
Setsuro Yamashita
Gordon Goro Yamaura
Hideo Heidi Yasui
Shigeo Yoshioka

Oregon, deliberately broke the curfew and gave himself up to a policeman.

When war broke out, Gordon Hirabayashi was a 25-year-old senior at the University of Washington. Despite pressure to comply from family and friends, he defied both the curfew and removal orders, turning himself over to the FBI in May of 1942. Hirabayashi was convicted of the violations in October and spent 24 months in jail.

In May 1943, the Hirabayashi curfew conviction was upheld by the U.S. Supreme Court in a 9-0 decision historian Roger Daniels calls a "grotesque example of how 'patriotism' can distort a judicial mind." In the written decision, Justice Harlan Fiske Stone acknowledged and condoned racial discrimination in the treatment of Japanese Americans, justifying it on the grounds of "dealing with the perils of war."

"When confronted with the option of obeying the government orders or to violate them, I had no choice but to disobey," wrote Hirabayashi years later. "My whole philosophy of life and motive to maintain good citizenship demanded that I uphold the constitutional guarantees."

The high court ruled the incarceration by the War Relocation Authority unconstitutional in *Mitsuye Endo vs. the United States* in December 1944. Endo was a California

> Gordon Hirabayashi defied both the curfew and removal orders, turning himself over to the FBI in May of 1942. Hirabayashi was convicted of the violations in October and spent 24 months in jail.

Nisei who challenged the government while confined in the camp at Topaz, Utah.

Most of the nation continued to live in virtual ignorance of America's concentration camps, except when incidents of violence in camps in California and Arizona were reported. The war was raging on two foreign fronts, and back home, the nation was pulling together in patriotism against the Axis. On the West Coast and in Washington, D.C., however, animosity against the incarcerated Japanese Americans remained high. Some complained the inmates were being "coddled," receiving better provisions than U.S.

enlisted men. "Food Is Hoarded for Japs in the U.S. While Americans in Nippon Are Tortured," blared one headline in the *Denver Post* in 1943.

Although the fifth column accusations had been thoroughly disproved, newspaper columnists and elected officials continued to yammer about disloyalty and potential sabotage. In 1943, when the question arose of whether to allow the Japanese back on the West Coast, Lieutenant General John L. DeWitt told the House Naval Affairs Committee: "A Jap's a Jap. They are a dangerous element, whether loyal or not. There's no way to determine their loyalty. It makes no difference whether he is an American citizen, theoretically. He is still a Japanese and you can't change him."

Washington state congressmen Henry Jackson and Warren Magnuson adamantly opposed a return of Japanese Americans to the West Coast.

III. STARTING OVER

Sports teams at Collins Playfield, 1947. Courtesy Virginia Boyd.

PART THREE

STARTING OVER

REJECTION, RESETTLEMENT

BEGINNING IN 1943, the War Relocation Authority promoted the idea of resettlement in the Midwest and on the East Coast through brochures with titles such as "Shuffle Off to Buffalo!" and "Cincinnati, a city for families." The brochures enticed camp residents with lists of job openings. A 1943 WRA pamphlet explained to potential resettlement communities that Japanese Americans were U.S. citizens and never guilty of any subversive acts. "They are merely a group of American residents who happened to have Japanese ancestors and who happened to be living in a potential combat zone shortly after the outbreak of war. All evidence available to the WRA indicates that the great majority of them are completely loyal to the United States."

College students were among the first to leave camp, followed by others who found work in areas outside the restricted zones. In 1943, Yoichi Matsuda got a job in the circulation department of the local paper in Twin Falls, just 25 miles from Minidoka. During the week, he stayed in town at the rented home of Reverend Emery Andrews, and visited his family each weekend in camp. From January 1945, Japanese were allowed to return to the West Coast.

The war ended soon after the bombing of Hiroshima and Nagasaki—another source of tragedy for the many Japanese Americans with relatives in Hiroshima. Minidoka was shut down in late October. The 2,000 remaining inmates were literally evicted from the camp. Water was cut off in the final days. One elderly man refused to move and was taken to the nearby town of Shoshone where camp officials gave him money for a train to Seattle. The man threw the money on the ground and walked back to camp. He was put on another train at Shoshone. In all 10 camps, 44,000 inmates remained until the bitter end.

While Americans were generous in their sympathy and goodwill toward Jews released from concentration camps in Europe, many turned an icy shoulder to returning Japanese Americans. Shigeo and Shigeko Nagaishi returned to their Seattle home to find the words "NO JAPS WANTED" painted crudely on the side of their house, and a pile of hate mail inside. One of the letters read in part: "Get out of town because there are too many true Americans that intend to get even with your race for what you have done to our boys. All I can say is get out of our city....We don't want Japs in the Northwest."

Some Nikkei didn't have homes to return to and faced a citywide housing shortage. They lived temporarily at the Seattle Buddhist Church and at the Japanese Language School, or doubled up in accommodations with family or friends. Others found that their businesses and homes had been vandalized and personal possessions stolen. Some families returning to

Headstones with Japanese names were toppled over in this Auburn cemetery, circa 1945. Reverend Emery Andrews photo, courtesy Bill Kunitsugu.

Bellevue found their homes had been burned to the ground. A fortunate few suffered minimal losses and could begin where they had left off.

Jobs were scarce at first. To many area employers, the idea of hiring the returning residents was repugnant. When Frank Arase wrote to his former employer asking for his old job back, an official with the Harrison Dye Works responded:

"I'm afraid you do not even remotely comprehend the attitude of the whole population of Seattle toward the Japanese at this time....It would indeed be business suicide for Mr. Spalding to hire a Japanese person in any capacity, as there would surely be an almost complete walkout. I am sure you would bump against the same stone wall should you try to obtain employment anywhere in Seattle at this time."

Issei were hit hardest by the uprooting, which ruined a half century of work and community effort. Many had suffered devastating financial losses from sold or abandoned businesses, homes, and belongings. Harsh living conditions in camp had taken a slow withering toll on many Issei, leaving little in reserve. The incarceration also subverted their authority within the family and the community. Although some Issei resumed their prewar professions in drugstores, apartment houses, groceries, hotels, and dry cleaners, many were too broken in spirit and body to begin again.

"I operated the Rainier Dye Works for 23 years," said one Issei man. "I am not accustomed to heavy outdoor work and gardening was too strenuous for me. I am uncertain of what I should do. I'm too old to start something new all over again."

Nihonmachi, as a result, was just a shell of its former self. Scattered businesses were revived, but the vibrancy of commercial and cultural life was destroyed. Coming of age in the 1960s and 1970s, Sansei were disinclined to go into small business, and as Nisei shopkeepers retired, more and more businesses closed their doors for good.

After the war, only a few farmers went back to Bellevue and the Puyallup and White River valleys. White farmers in Auburn and Kent had formed the Pearl Harbor League to prevent the return of Nikkei farmers. Mitsuko and John Hamakami returned from Minidoka to find their farm along the Green River in shambles. All the equipment they had left behind was gone. "We had to start from scratch, just like everyone else," Mitsuko Hamakami told the *Northwest Nikkei* newspaper. Because their tractor had been stolen, they started tilling the land with a horse-drawn plow.

Farmers were also stymied by boycotts and bans. Local Teamsters Union president Dave Beck campaigned to prevent Japanese from selling their crops in Seattle's Produce Row. Reverend Andrews and other sympathetic Christian ministers acted as middlemen to sell the produce. As they had before the war, most unions excluded Nikkei workers.

Hostile attitudes were ameliorated by the well-publicized heroics of the 442nd. Among many other honors, the 442nd marched in a parade down Constitution Avenue in Washington, D.C., in 1946. WRA representatives spoke to anti-Japanese groups about the Nisei war record, sometimes quoting the words of General Joseph Stillwell, commander of American forces in China, Burma, and India: "They bought an awful hunk of America with their blood....You're damn right those Nisei boys have a place in the American heart, now and forever. We cannot allow a single injustice to be done to the Nisei without defeating the purposes for which we fought."

The postwar period underscored the ascendancy of the Nisei. With the help of the WRA Center in Seattle, Nisei found work as file clerks, typists, laborers, porters, janitors, and workers in hotels and hospitals. Nisei job seekers found federal and local government agencies more receptive than private companies, but even those employers began to loosen restrictions. Women worked as maids and seamstresses and also took the opportunity to go to college and find professional work. Nisei veterans

Japanese community queen contest, 1950. Courtesy Shigeko Uno.

Lotus Skyliners, a popular band, board a bus for a concert tour, August 1955. Royal C. Crooks photo.

went to college on the G.I. Bill.

The elaborate social and community structure—*kenjinkai,* the Japanese Association—weakened after the war from reduced membership and geographic dispersal. But a community core endured. Churches played a significant role in the recovery as the community's social and spiritual centers. Sports teams revived, including numerous bowling leagues at the favorite local hangout, Main Bowl, and later, Imperial Lanes. Another Nisei haunt was the Spanish Castle, a dance hall on Pacific Highway South, where young people danced to the tunes of community bands like the Lotus Skyliners. Nisei kept informed through the *Northwest Times,* first published in 1947 by Budd Fukei. Two Japanese-language papers started up after the war: the *Hokubei Hochi* and the *Seihoku Nippo.* Veterans formed the Nisei Veterans Committee. Most of the Japanese American churches—St. Peter's Episcopal, Blaine Methodist, Japanese Baptist, and Seattle Buddhist—sponsored Boy Scout troops. The Seattle Buddhist Boy Scouts formed a drum-and-bugle corps that became renowned for its performances in Seafair and Fourth of July parades.

The drive to assimilate was even stronger than before the war. Many Nisei believed they had been imprisoned because Japanese

Seiji Hanada displays produce in front of his Pike Place Market stall in August 1963. Hanada was one of the few Japanese Americans to resume truck farming after the war. Joseph Scaylea photo, Seattle Times, *courtesy Mrs. Seiji Hanada.*

Americans stood out as different from other Americans. Ichiro's girlfriend, Emi, explains in Okada's *No-No Boy:* "It's because we're American and because we're Japanese and sometimes the two don't mix. It's all right to be German and American or Italian and American or Russian and American but, as things turned out, it wasn't all right to be Japanese and American. You had to be one or the other."

The Japanese Language School reopened in 1956 with Iwao Matsushita as its volunteer principal. But Japanese culture and language, once a source of great pride,

were considered by many in the younger generation with a mixture of shame and aversion.

The Japanese population in Washington state dwindled from 14,400 before the war to 9,700 in 1950, a drop of 34 percent. In Seattle, the population decreased from a high of 7,000 in 1940 to 5,800 in 1950. The community was still clustered along Yesler and Jackson from 4th to 23rd avenues, though many of their former residences had been occupied by Seattle's growing black community. "No non-Caucasian" clauses were still written into property deeds in areas of Capitol Hill, Laurelhurst, and the University District, but those barriers slowly began to fall.

BREAKING BARRIERS

REPUDIATED IN CAMP, the JACL rebounded. The relocation of Nikkei to the Midwest and East Coast strengthened the organization and made it truly national in scope. The JACL lobby in Washington, D.C., under Mike Masaoka, was instrumental in passing several pieces of legislation benefiting Japanese Americans. In 1948, President Truman signed the Japanese Evacuation Claims Act, which paid a total of $37 million, or just nine cents to the dollar of the estimated $400 million in actual losses. Former in-mates couldn't claim lost wages or other damages, and the claims process was slow and burdensome.

Another more sweeping legislative victory was the passage of the McCarran-Walter Immigration Act of 1952, which lifted the restriction against Issei becoming naturalized U.S. citizens. The Immigration Act of 1965 completely eliminated quotas of national origin, effectively overturning the odious Immigration Act of 1924. It wasn't until 1966, after several attempts, that Washington state's Alien Land Law was repealed.

A new generation brought even more changes. Like millions of other American young people, Sansei were swept up in the tumult of the 1960s and early 1970s: the civil rights movement, counterculture, protests against the Vietnam War, and the questioning of materialistic goals. Profoundly influenced by Martin Luther King, Jr., and the Black Power movement of the late 1960s, Sansei no longer chose to "melt" into the American pot but began to discover their own ethnic heritage as Japanese Americans and, more broadly, as "Asian Americans." Seattle was unique in the number of Japanese, Chinese, and Filipinos living in the same neighborhoods and attending the same schools. Asians in integrated school districts took their cue from African Americans, adopting

their music, fashion, and sense of indignation. Cleveland and Franklin high schools, for instance, had large percentages of blacks and Asians. At the same time, Sansei explored their cultural roots by forming *taiko* drum groups, studying Japanese language, and traveling to Japan.

The movement also spawned Asian American Studies courses and student organizations at the University of Washington, Washington State University, and other colleges throughout the country. The courses examined the long history of Japanese and Asians in America and challenged the government and JACL version of the events of the 1940s. The history revealed that Japanese and other Asians were among the earliest non-Indian settlers of the American West and, from the very beginning, experienced racist hatred and discrimination from the white majority. Seen in this vein, the wartime incarceration was not simply an isolated blunder of judgment on the part of local and federal authorities, but the culmination of nearly a century of hate-mongering, immigration restrictions, segregation, and discrimination in housing, marriage, employment, and education.

Questioning the past triggered a call for political action in the form of demonstrations to preserve the former Nihonmachi, now known as the International District, which

The Japanese American community keeps in touch via the North American Post.

immigrants from China, Japan, and the Philippines had long called home. By coalescing, the groups found they had more clout. In the early 1970s, activists protested against the building of the Kingdome stadium and in the process won concessions from local and federal authorities to fund low-income housing and social services for the neighborhood's elderly, non-English-speaking residents.

At about the same time, demonstrators at Seattle Central Community College demanded the addition of Asian American Studies courses, and Asian American faculty, counselors, and administrators at the college. Although 10 percent of the student body was Asian, none of the 90 college administrators was Asian.

Today, many of these same activists have entered the mainstream of government and politics. "Politically, the Asian community grew up," says Gary Iwamoto, an attorney and activist who took part in many of the protests. "Before, it was us against them....Now if you're protesting about things wrong with the School Board, Jan Kumasaka is a member of the board. If you think the city is messing up, you've got people you know working for the mayor and who are actually on the City Council."

Kip Tokuda represents southeast Seattle in the Washington State Legislature. Richard Ishikawa is a King County Superior Court judge, and Carolyn Kimi Kondo, Eileen Kato, and Ron Mamiya sit on other court benches.

The renewed interest in politics, heritage, and identity also revived Asian American newspapers. Founded in 1974, the biweekly *International Examiner* paved the way for more recent publications: the *Northwest Asian Weekly* and another Japanese community newspaper, the *Northwest Nikkei,* now merged with the *North American Post.*

Increasing opportunities meant greater economic freedom and a migration to the suburbs and other neighborhoods previously off-limits for Asians. Japanese Americans achieved the highest high school graduation rate of any ethnic group. Nisei and Sansei also made great strides in a broad range of professions from engineering to medicine to business to government. Some, such as television anchor Wendy Tokuda, former Microsoft executive Scott Oki, Seattle Mariners executive Paul Isaki, and the late schoolteacher Aki Kurose, rose to the top of their fields. By 1970, more than half the population were in white-collar jobs, though many earned less money than white professionals with the same level of education and training.

Their success swung the pendulum of public perception of Japanese Americans from one of hatred and resentment to admiration. Asian Americans were dubbed the "model minority" by the media, a stereotype that masked the growing complexity and diversity of the Asian community. Other versions of the stereotype categorized Japanese Americans as quiet, obedient, and "nice."

As more Japanese Americans joined the mainstream, a growing number split off to pursue more unorthodox careers in music and the arts. Sansei artists Patti Warashina, Roger Shimomura, and others followed in the footsteps of Seattle Nisei artists John Matsudaira, Frank Okada, Paul Horiuchi, and George Tsutakawa, who achieved fame regionally and nationally. Tsutakawa in particular was prodigious well into the 1980s, with 75 major sculptures in the United States, Canada, and Japan. His bronze fountain sculptures inspired by Tibetan rock piles became his signature work.

The 1980s seemed especially fertile for Japanese American writers and actors. Ken Mochizuki wrote the script for the acclaimed film *Beacon Hill Boys* about growing up in Seattle. Tomo Shoji, a spunky Nisei woman, did a series of one-woman shows about her experiences to packed houses at the Nippon Kan Theater. Playwright Gary Iwamoto's musical *Miss Minidoka 1943* was performed in 1986 by the already well-established Northwest Asian American Theater.

A few years later, Nisei actors Harry Fujita and Tama Tokuda earned rave reviews for their poignant, dead-on portrayal of an estranged Nisei couple in Phillip Kan Gotanda's play, *The Wash*.

Poets and prose writers also emerged, chief among them, *No-No Boy* author John Okada. Okada had died in 1971 with his book virtually unknown outside of a small circle of Asian American friends. After his death, the book's status slowly grew and it became a regular text in American literature and Asian American Studies courses at the university level. Ken Mochizuki wrote about

Young people demonstrate for low-income housing for Asian elderly, early 1970s.

Uwajimaya

Nihonmachi may be gone forever, but the spirit of immigrant entrepreneurship lives on in Seattle's most recognizable Japanese American landmark, Uwajimaya department store.

Fujimatsu Moriguchi, a native of Yawatahama, Japan, began the business in 1928 in Tacoma. It was retail at its most basic and intimate level: Moriguchi sold fresh *kamaboko* (fish cakes) from the back of a truck to Japanese farmers, loggers, fishermen, and railroad workers.

After the war and imprisonment in a concentration camp in Tule Lake, California, the Moriguchis relocated to Seattle, where the once thriving Nihonmachi had withered to a handful of Japanese-owned businesses. The store slowly grew, aided by the influx of Japanese women married to American servicemen and, a few decades later, the arrival of thousands of Southeast Asian refugees. Uwajimaya also began importing food and gifts directly from Japan, attracting more non-Japanese customers, and under the leadership of son Tomio Moriguchi, the store added food from other Asian countries.

In 1970, Uwajimaya moved to a new building at 6th Avenue South and South King Street and, in 1978, expanded again to a total of 36,000 square feet—far and away the largest retailer in the neighborhood. Known affectionately in the Japanese community as "Waji's," the familiar white stucco building with the blue-tiled roof now occupies an entire city block in the International District. Uwajimaya also has stores in Bellevue, Washington, and Beaverton, Oregon, and plans a major expansion of its Seattle store in the late 1990s. Now one of the top 150 privately held companies in Washington state, Uwajimaya boasts annual retail sales of more than $20 million and wholesale sales of more than $30 million.

As many third- and fourth-generation Japanese Americans have chosen a broad range of careers and other places to live, Uwajimaya serves as kind of community anchor—an important link to the immigrant past and a symbol of a new generation's success.

camp experience from a child's perspective in the award-winning *Baseball Saved Us* and subsequent children's stories. Poets Sharon Hashimoto, Lonny Kaneko, and James Mitsui are frequently published in local and national anthologies.

Not forgotten in the pursuit of professional and financial success were the sacrifices of the community's aging Issei generation. Besides the campaign for redress, perhaps the greatest community effort after the war was the building of the Japanese nursing home, Keiro. In just a few years, organizers raised millions of dollars, tapping Nikkei community support to build a 150-bed nursing home that was sensitive to the language, cultural, and dietary needs of Japanese elderly. Opened in 1976, Keiro is still the focus of many community charity drives and volunteer activities. In early 1998, the Keiro organizers, now called Nikkei Concerns, opened another senior housing building for aging Nisei, at the southern edge of the International District. The Nikkei Manor features "assisted living" that includes meals, physical therapy, communal activities, and other assistance.

Nisei have remained active in such organizations as the Nisei Veterans Committee, the JACL, churches, a widows' and widowers' support group called Tomo no Kai, the First Hill Lions, and other groups. The

Artist Patti Warashina, 1991. Dean Wong photo.

Nihongo Gakko continues to hold classes, making it the oldest operating Japanese language school on the U.S. mainland.

QUEST FOR REDRESS

THE CIVIL RIGHTS ERA also inspired the movement to right the wrong of the wartime incarceration. The idea for monetary reparations was first raised by Nisei Edison Uno, a lecturer at San Francisco State University. Uno introduced a redress resolution at the 1970 JACL national convention, calling for government payment of $400 million for the revitalization of ethnic studies, museums, and community centers for all minorities.

Over the next two decades, Seattle Nisei and Sansei played a key leadership role in the push for individual monetary redress for Japanese Americans imprisoned during the Second World War. Nisei engineer Henry Miyatake began researching the idea in 1972 along with Shosuke Sasaki, Ken Nakano, Chuck Kato, Mike Nakata, Tomio Moriguchi, and John Takizawa. By 1974 a Seattle plan was developed by the local chapter of the JACL.

Initially, the proposal was roundly criticized and feared. Nisei reasoned that no amount of money could compensate them for the loss and suffering of 30 years past. Besides, why reopen old wounds and expose the community to a public (white) backlash? California senator S.I. Hayakawa was among the proposal's most vociferous critics—as was the national JACL.

The idea gained momentum in 1976 when Seattle activists succeeded in getting President Gerald Ford to issue an official apology and rescind Executive Order 9066, and again in 1978, when more than 2,000 Japanese Americans converged on the Puyallup Fairgrounds, the site of the "assembly center." Seattle's "Day of Remembrance," the brainchild of Chinese American writer Frank Chin, was the first of many emotional pilgrimages on the West Coast.

At the urging of Seattle activists, Congressman Mike Lowry of Washington state introduced the first redress bill during his freshman year in Congress in 1979, calling for $15,000 and a per diem individual payment to each former camp inmate. Although the bill died in committee, an alternative bill became law in 1980, establishing the fact-finding Commission on Wartime Relocation and Internment of Civilians. This legislation was supported in Congress by Hawaii senators Daniel Inouye and Spark Matsunaga, California congressmen Norman Mineta and Robert Matsui, and California senator S.I. Hayakawa.

Gordon Hirabayashi (center with bow tie) surrounded by his legal team, 1988. Dean Wong photo.

Shosuke Sasaki, Henry Miyatake, Chuck Kato, Mike Nakata, and Ken Nakano were instrumental in the formation of the 1974 redress plan. John Esaki photo, courtesy JACL.

Bea Kiyohara with daughters Joby and Yoko Shimomura make the Day of Remembrance pilgrimage to Puyallup in 1978. Courtesy International Examiner.

U.S. Assistant Deputy Attorney General James P. Turner presents a redress check to 107-year-old Frank Yatsu at the Nisei Veterans Hall, Seattle, October 1990. Courtesy Akio Yanagihara.

The commission visited selected cities, hearing testimony from more than 750 individuals. At first regarded as a "sell-out" by activists demanding monetary redress, the commission hearings publicly aired the wrongs of the incarceration for the first time since the end of the war and served as an emotional catharsis for Nisei and Issei who testified.

"The government we trusted, the country we loved, the nation to which we pledged loyalty, betrayed us, had turned against us," Fife Nisei veteran Robert T. Mizukami told commission members.

The question again arose as to why the Nisei failed to protest their unjust treatment. Gordon Hirabayashi likened the experience to rape. "Somehow, like the other rape victims, you're the victim of it, but you feel degraded by it," he told the *Seattle Times*. "And you feel ashamed. It takes you a while to come out and say I was done in and we shouldn't do it any more. You

sort of want to keep it quiet."

For many Nisei, the time had come to speak out. Public testimony provoked similar conversations in Japanese American homes as parents told children in detail for the first time about their wartime experiences. At the conclusion of the hearings, the commission recommended payment of $20,000 for each camp resident.

By this time the national JACL had revived the redress cause with the formation of the National JACL Redress Committee in 1978 and, over the next 10 years, raised $1.5 million to fund a public educational program on the camp experience and a vigorous lobbying effort for redress in every state of the union. In Seattle, the Washington Coalition on Redress, composed of 16 major Nikkei organizations and churches, was organized in 1980 by Cherry Kinoshita. The entire Washington state congressional delegation lined up in support of the redress bill.

Masao Takahashi, Kusunosuke Kino, and Tak Mitsui testify at Seattle Central Community College in 1980 before the Commission on Wartime Relocation and Internment of Civilians. Stan Shikuma photo.

Yet another avenue of monetary redress was pursued by William Hohri and the National Council for Japanese American Redress (NCJAR) via a class-action lawsuit. With strong support from a core of Seattle activists, NCJAR sought $27 billion in compensation for Nikkei losses and the gross violation of their constitutional rights. Although ultimately rejected, the suit was instrumental in raising national consciousness of the injustice of the camps.

Also during the 1980s, Hirabayashi, Minoru Yasui, and Fred Korematsu filed *coram nobis* briefs, seeking to overturn their convictions for violating the curfew and removal orders. New evidence was uncovered indicating the U.S. government had suppressed evidence in the Supreme Court trials of 1943 and 1944. Specifically, government attorneys had unlawfully withheld information that revealed there was no "military necessity" and that racism was the underlying reason for the expulsion of Japanese Americans. Hirabayashi was vindicated when his convictions, for violating exclusion orders and the curfew, were vacated in 1986 and 1988 respectively. The convictions for Korematsu and Yasui were also overturned.

Of local note, the legal teams for the three petitioners included Japanese American attorneys from Seattle, who volunteered thousands of

Junkoh Harui (center) and neighbors protest distribution of racist literature on Bainbridge Island, 1991. Dean Wong photo.

hours of time for legal research and preparation, and lawyers of many different ethnic backgrounds.

The Civil Liberties Act, signed by President Ronald Reagan in 1988, acknowledged the commission's findings that the imprisonment of Japanese Americans was "motivated largely by racial prejudice and wartime hysteria, and failure of political leadership." Besides a payment of $20,000 to each surviving inmate, the act established a fund to educate the public. In a ceremony on Octo-

ber 14, 1990, in Seattle, 107-year-old Frank Yatsu and four other Issei over the age of 100 were presented with redress checks and a presidential apology.

Washington state had made similar amends in 1983 by paying $5,000 each to 38 Japanese Americans who had lost their state jobs after the outbreak of World War II. In 1986, the 26 Nisei school clerks who had been forced to resign before their incarceration were compensated with $5,000 payments from the state.

WHAT THE FUTURE HOLDS

IN THE LATE 1990S, the Nikkei community in Seattle is unalterably in flux. More than half of all Sansei and Yonsei (fourth generation) are marrying partners of a different race. Unlike the Chinese and Filipinos, few Japanese from Japan have immigrated in recent years. The population is still growing, reaching 34,366 in Washington state in 1990, but Japanese Americans comprise just 16 percent of the total Asian population, compared to 26 percent in 1980.

While young people have joined churches, the JACL, and Seattle Sansei (the Sansei arm of the Nisei Veterans Committee), many remain apathetic toward issues of culture and politics and seem to have little in common besides a fondness for Japanese food. It's hardly surprising considering that Sansei were raised in a vastly different world from their Nisei parents. No longer confined to an ethnic ghetto, they grew up in many settings—among predominantly white friends and neighbors, among Asians, among several different races.

Even so, there are fresh signs of community strength. Gary Iwamoto puts it this way: "Culturally, the Japanese American community is

Kimi Egashira and great-grandson Kenji Thomas Egashira, 1991. Dean Wong photo.

disappearing, but politically we're as strong as ever. If you don't believe that, then how did we get the redress bill passed?"

Other issues continue to unify the community in anger and action. Racism still simmers just below the surface. As Japan grew again into an economic power in the 1980s, racial and cultural stereotyping stormed back into the mass media. When Sony bought Columbia Pictures, *Newsweek* magazine pictured the Statue of Liberty in a kimono beside the headline "Japan Invades Hollywood." Media coverage of the 50th anniversary of Pearl Harbor included numerous references to Japan's trade policy with the U.S. as an "economic Pearl Harbor."

The "Japan bashing" played on the fears of the American public. In the late 1980s, polls showed more Americans perceived the Japanese economic challenge as a greater threat to U.S. security than the Soviet military. Because many Americans did not differentiate Asian Americans from Asian nationals, the anti-Japanese mood reflected on Japanese Americans and Asian Americans. The late teacher Aki Kurose recalled a child being transferred out of her first-grade class at Laurelhurst Elementary School because his mother didn't like the Japanese.

Similarly, Japanese Americans were hurt by broader attacks on Asian Americans. In the 1997 Democratic Party fund-raising controversy, media reports and Democratic National Committee auditors lumped together Asian Americans with Asian nationals accused of illegal campaign contributions and undue influence. Some analysts believed the scandal caused the Clinton administration to drop from consideration two Asian American candidates for Cabinet posts, including former U.S. congressman Norm Mineta of California for Secretary of Transportation.

More insidious is the evidence that many Americans have learned nothing from past mistakes. In another poll taken in California by the Field Institute, a third of all respondents believed the U.S. government was right to have sent Japanese Americans to concentration camps during the war.

The 50th Pearl Harbor anniversary provided a forum for the ignorant (and frequently voiced) argument that Japanese American redress was undeserved considering that the Japanese government has never compensated American victims of World War II. The problem with that argument is, of course, that the incarceration of Japanese Americans was something inflicted by the U.S. government *on its own citizens.*

Grace Hiranaka of Kent wrote a reply to these critics in the *Auburn Globe News:* "I feel a great sadness that in this country of mine, there are still people who judge me by the color of my skin and hair and the shape of my eyes, and blame me for what happened at Pearl Harbor."

Racist talk can and does escalate into violence. In 1983, Vincent Chin was beaten to death in Detroit by an autoworker and his stepson. The men mistook Chin, a Chinese American, for a Japanese national. Racist groups such as the Aryan Nations and skinheads, though hardly prevalent, have gained popular currency.

Equally disturbing was the way other minorities—especially Arab Americans—were victimized when tensions heightened between the United States and Middle Eastern countries. When Iranian extremists held 52 Americans hostage for 444 days from 1979 to 1981, Iranians living in America endured threats, hate mail, and beatings. During the 1991 Persian Gulf War, Iraqis (and Saudi Arabians and Kuwaitis) living here experienced similar hostility. In Great Britain, there was talk of detaining Iraqi nationals.

Other discrimination is more subtle. In the workplace, Japanese Americans and other Asian Americans find themselves bumping against a "glass ceiling" when it comes to promotions into managerial or executive positions. Stereotypes of the hardworking make-no-waves Asian American are used against them. Asians have made impressive progress, but "it's like pedaling uphill," says former Seattle School Board member Al Sugiyama. "As soon as you stop pedaling you start going down. In order to continue that progress, we have to continue pumping that bike."

Japanese Americans are applying lessons learned from the redress movement to combat these injustices and, more broadly, to promote civil and human rights both at home and abroad.

In the early and mid-1990s, 50-year anniversaries of wartime experiences spurred a drive to record and preserve the past. The Wing Luke Asian Museum's 1992 exhibition on Japanese Americans, *Executive Order 9066: 50 Years*

Nisei veteran Tosh Tokunaga during Pearl Harbor anniversary ceremony, 1991. Dean Wong photo.

"I think I have been mad
for many, many years.
You get over it, but you never
forget it. If people say they've
forgotten it, I think they aren't
being very truthful."

Before and 50 Years After received national attention for its community-based exploration of history. During the exhibit planning, Nisei and Issei shared long-held family photos and artifacts and told their stories as never before.

One of the discoveries of exhibition researchers was a time capsule of artifacts in the basement of the Panama Hotel, in the heart of the former Nihonmachi. There, next to an abandoned Japanese bathhouse, were photographs, magazines, books, kitchen utensils, suitcases, furniture, and trunks of clothing left behind and never reclaimed by Japanese Americans in the haste of their departure for Camp Harmony in the spring of 1942. Pressed white shirts looked as if they were ready to wear. The storage room had an eerie feeling of time standing still.

The chronicling of the local Japanese American experience has been advanced by community historian Ed Suguro, writing in the *Northwest Nikkei* newspaper, as well as by the Densho Project, which is collecting photographs and video interviews with community members for inclusion in a digital archive, and by projects supported by the Civil Liberties Public Education Fund, which was part of the redress legislation. New books include Louis Fiset's *Imprisoned Apart,* about the wartime correspondence of an Issei couple, Iwao and Hanaye Matsushita.

The Matsushitas were imprisoned in separate camps for more than two years before they were reunited in Minidoka.

Nationally, interest in Japanese American history and culture has never been greater, with dozens of new books on the subject and the establishment of the Japanese American National Museum in Los Angeles in 1992. In the same year, a campaign to build a national monument to Japanese Americans in Washington, D.C., got under way.

RETURN TO MINIDOKA

MORE THAN 50 YEARS have passed since the beginning of World War II and the Japanese community's defining trauma. Although the healing process has begun for Japanese Americans, wartime fractures still run deep.

Efforts to recognize "no-no boys" and draft resisters have met with fierce opposition from some Nisei military veterans. While many Nikkei have become more vocal about the camp experience, many more have remained silent. Many Issei and Nisei have gone to their graves in silence, buried with their anguish and disappointment—profound feelings of failure that can never be quantified or redressed.

Those who have shared their

stories speak of lasting psychological wounds. For many years, author and psychologist Monica Sone repressed the "guilt, self-hate and fear" she felt from the experience. At a 1980 symposium, Sone recalled: "I experienced all that hate which had poured out from the public and the government officials as a death wish upon us. That message had sunk deeply inside me."

The experience may be gone but it will never be forgotten. "I think I have been mad for many, many years," says Yukiko Miyake. "You get over it, but you never forget it. If people say they've forgotten it, I think they aren't being very truthful."

In recent years, Nisei have returned to the scene of the crime, Minidoka, some to reminisce and meet old friends, others to take stock, to mend. Sansei have joined the pilgrimages to bear witness to the past.

Minidoka, they find, has undergone a dramatic transformation. After the war, the camp land reverted to the U.S. Bureau of Reclamation and was given as homesteads to returning war veterans (Japanese Americans were forbidden from settling on the site, despite their efforts to cultivate the land). Most of the barracks were razed, but some were transported intact to nearby towns and renovated into family homes or quarters for migrant farm workers. The camp hospital was sold to a large shepherding family and was moved north to the foothills of the Sawtooth Mountains.

Today, much of the countryside is covered by cultivated fields, thanks in large part to the incarcerated Japanese and Japanese Americans who first worked the land. The former desert has been transformed into placid fields of vegetables, watered by long, rolling sprinklers. Recently harvested hay, golden in color, lies stacked in rectangular or circular ricks at the ends of fields.

"When I left camp for the last time," recalls Yoshisada Kawai, "I looked back and saw the entire ground; when we came it was nothing but wilderness, but now, because of our labor, it had become a beautiful green field."

Near the former entrance to Minidoka, the irrigation canal still swells with water, but all that apparently remains of the camp are the ruins of a stone wall and chimney of the guardhouse. The dust is still there, as fine and light as flour, but it is beneath the surface, along the sides of the roads near clumps of sagebrush. The sky is big, streaked with high clouds, descending all around to the distant horizon.

Another visitor, May Sasaki, found her mind drifting back to an earlier time, when she was a girl of seven or eight. "I couldn't remember because...all the barracks were down. I couldn't decide where Block 14 was. And my husband...walked to the fence and showed me. And I remember [standing] there and

Present-day Minidoka. Michelle Kumata illustration.

Seattle's only youth taiko group, Tsunami Taiko, performs on the Seattle waterfront in 1994. The drummers range in age from 11 to 18. I.H. Kuniyuki photo.

looking. And then the tears started rolling down because I guess you think, gosh, I didn't realize what it was until after…. And I was so young not to realize it and I'm grateful to my parents who made that life bearable."

On a recent summer afternoon, Fumi Matsuda, a former Minidoka inmate who lives in nearby Twin Falls, accompanied several young pilgrims to the camp site. She stood near the spot by the guardhouse where buses used to stop to take prisoners into town and pointed to the nearly deserted fields where there once was a small city. "Over there is where the hospital used to be," she said, motioning to an old shed. "And over there"—indicating a clump of trees on a slight hill that appeared to be a mile or two away —"is where we used to live. In Block 15."

As the visitors prepared to leave, Matsuda pointed into the distance again, to where there had once been a cemetery for Issei bachelors and others who died while in camp. After the war, their remains were taken back to Seattle for burial in family plots, and when the land at Hunt was abandoned and then parceled out to homesteaders, these former grave sites were tilled into the soil. The soil, as it turned out, was ideal for agriculture. With sustained irrigation over subsequent decades, the dust of Minidoka became as fertile as any farmland in the Northwest, rivaling Washington's Yakima Valley and the Palouse.

SELECTED BIBLIOGRAPHY

Chin, Doug, and Peter Bacho. "The Origins of the International District." Seattle: *International Examiner,* November 21, 1984.

Chuman, Frank F. *The Bamboo People: The Law and Japanese Americans.* Del Mar, California: Publishers Inc., 1976.

Daniels, Roger. *Asian America: Chinese and Japanese in the United States since 1850.* Seattle: University of Washington Press, 1989.

The Densho Project, a Seattle-based organization that is constructing a digital archive of personal visual histories and historic photographs.

Fiset, Louis. *Imprisoned Apart: The World War II Correspondence of an Issei Couple.* Seattle: University of Washington Press, 1998.

Fisher, Anne Reeploeg. *Exile of a Race.* Seattle: F and T Publishers, 1965.

Fukuhara, Francis. *Uncommon American Patriots* (booklet). Seattle: Nisei Veterans Committee, 1991.

Ito, Kazuo. *Issei: A History of Japanese Immigrants in North America.* Seattle: Executive Committee for Publication of *Issei,* 1973.

McKivor, June Mukai, editor. *Kenjiro Nomura: The George and Betty Nomura Collection* (museum catalog). Seattle: Wing Luke Asian Museum, 1991.

Miyamoto, Frank. *Social Solidarity among the Japanese in Seattle.* Seattle: University of Washington, 1939.

Nishinoiri, John. *Japanese Farms in Washington* (master's thesis). Seattle: University of Washington, 1926.

Nomura, Gail M. "Washington's Asian/Pacific American Communities," in *Peoples of Washington: Perspectives on Cultural Diversity,* Sid White and S.E. Solberg, editors. Pullman: Washington State University Press, 1989.

Okada, John. *No-No Boy.* Rutherford, Vermont: Charles E. Tuttle, 1957.

Rademaker, John. *The Ecological Position of the Japanese Farmers in the State of Washington* (Ph.D. dissertation). Seattle: University of Washington, 1939.

Sone, Monica. *Nisei Daughter.* Boston: Little, Brown and Co., 1953.

Takami, David. *Shared Dreams: A History of Asian and Pacific Americans in Washington State.* Seattle: Washington State Centennial Commission, 1989.

Takezawa, Yasuko I. *Breaking the Silence: Ethnicity and the Quest for Redress among Japanese Americans* (Ph.D. dissertation). Seattle: University of Washington, 1989.

Tsushima, Asaichi. *Pre-WWII History of Japanese Pioneers in the Clearing and Development of Land in Bellevue.* Bellevue: private publisher, 1952.

Tsutakawa, Mayumi, editor. *They Painted from Their Hearts: Pioneer Asian American Artists.* Seattle: Wing Luke Asian Museum and University of Washington Press, 1994.

Tsutakawa, Mayumi, and Alan Chong Lau, editors. *Turning Shadows into Light: Art and Culture of the Northwest's Early Asian/Pacific Community.* Seattle: Young Pine Press, 1982.

United States Department of the Interior. *People in Motion: The Postwar Adjustment of the Evacuated Japanese Americans.* Washington, D.C., 1947.

War Relocation Authority. *Final Report: Japanese Evacuation from the West Coast.* Washington, D.C.: Government Printing Office, 1942.

Weglyn, Michi. *Years of Infamy: The Untold Story of America's Concentration Camps.* New York: William Morrow and Co., Inc., 1976.

Yamaguchi, Jack. *This Was Minidoka.* Nagaoka, Japan: Nagai Printing Co., Ltd., 1989.

ACKNOWLEDGMENTS

This book and the museum exhibition it was based on would not have been possible without the cooperation of many people and organizations who generously shared their stories, photographs, documents, artifacts, knowledge, and support:

Executive Order 9066: 50 Years Before and 50 Years After

PROJECT CHAIRS

Research: Sally Yamasaki
Design: Michelle Kumata
Writing: David Takami
Project Assistant: Harry Fujita
Publicity: Leslie Matsuda
Fund-raising: Hannah Yamasaki

Divided Destiny: A History of Japanese Americans in Seattle

WING LUKE ASIAN MUSEUM PROJECT STAFF

Executive Director: Ron Chew
Associate Director: Beth Takekawa
Development Director: Diane Wah
Director of Education and Programs: Charlene Mano
Education Associate: Kristi Woo
Curator of Collections: Ruth Vincent
Collections Associate: Bob Fisher
Public Relations Manager: Melanie Apostol
Membership Coordinator and Book Distribution: Jennie Pu
Programming Coordinator: Byron Au Yong

Frank Abe
Paul Aburano
Sharon Aburano
Mary Akamine
Jim Akutsu
Herbert Amano
American Airlines
Pauline Asaba
Bainbridge Island Historical Society, Lucille Galbraith
Sally Jane Beal
Daniel Benson
Blaine Memorial United Methodist Church
Virginia Boyd
Leslie and Tom Chaffey
Masako Chikamura
Takeshi Chikamura
Natsuko Chinn
Bruce Christopherson
Harry Conrad
Mary Ann Cunanan
Roger Daniels
Densho Project
Des Moines Historical Society, Melanie Draper
Eydie Calderon Detera
Lisa Ely
Carmen Espanol
Harue Farrington
Louis Fiset
Kit Freudenberg
Frank Fujii
Gloria Fujii
Kei Fujimura
Harry Fujino
Becky Fukuda
Tami Fukuda
David Fukuhara
Mas Fukuhara

Carey Quan Gelernter
Howard Giske
Tim Gojio
Trevor and Jean Greenwood
Jennifer Hall
Glen Hamada
Jeff Hanada
Seiji Hanada
Junkoh Harui
Michiyo Hashimoto
Tok Hirotaka
Tak Hori
Hideo Hoshide
Danny Howe
Yukiko Howell
Ayako Hurd
Sumi Ikeda
Tom Ikeda
Tsuguo Ikeda
Victor and Mary Ikeda
David Imanaka
Tim Imanaka
K/P Corporation, Rick Fickel
International Examiner
Roy Inui
Marie Ishii
Shig and Haru Ishikawa
Alice Ito
Tosh Ito
Sachi and Kanichi Iwami
Gary Iwamoto
Kats Iwamura
Laura Iwasaki
JAE Awards, Polly Shigaki
Japanese American Citizens League (Seattle)
Japanese Congregational Church
Japanese Language School
Japanese American National Museum, Gary Kawaguchi

JKM Productions
Jan Johnson
C. Kamiyama
Lillie Kanegae
Tsuyako Kaneko
Tetsuden Kashima
Shiro and Lou Kashino
Harriett Kashiwada
Lily Kato
Marcia Kato
Kunitaro Kawaguchi family
Rod Kawakami
Sally Kazama
King County Cultural
   Development Fund
Cherry Kinoshita
Shigeko Kitamoto
Bea Kiyohara
Mas Koba
Kaz and Amy Kobayashi
KOMO-TV
Betty Komura
Flo Koura
Vic Kubo
Jack Kudo
Rick Kumasaka
Irene Kuniyuki
Aki Kurose
Jim Linardos
Debbie Louie
Machiko Maeda
Sharon Maeda
Zentaro Maekawa
Ron Magden
Yoshi and George Mamiya
Master Press, Ron Shigeno
Fumi Masunaga
Yoichi and Fumi Matsuda
Tak and Mitzi Matsui
Fran Matsuoka

Tom Takeo Matsuoka
June McKivor
Michiko Mitsuoka
Norio and Laurette Mitsuoka
Yuki Miyake
Frank Miyamoto
Ken Mochizuki
Steve Momii
J. Morehouse
Mac Mori
Tomio Moriguchi
Dr. James Morishima
Motoda Foundation
Ralph Munro
Aya Murakami
Masa Murakami
Richard Murakami
Pam Muramatsu
Museum of History and
   Industry
Leslie Nakagawa
Sheri Nakashima
Don Nakata
Diane Narasaki
National Archives—Pacific
   Northwest, Joyce Justice
National Japanese American
   Historical Society
Frank Natsuhara
Amy Nikaitani
Martha Nishitani
Jackie Nogaki
Gail Nomura
Hideo Nomura
Koji Norikane
Mary Norikane
Pat Norikane
North American Post
Northwest Nikkei
Cano Numoto

Katashi Oita
Gene Okamura
Frank Okimoto
Chizuko Omori
Francis Osawa
Pacific Components, Inc.,
   Dan Mar
Wingate Packard
Marilyn Ridge
Kimi Sakai
Misao Sakamoto
Lilly Sako
Melanie Sako
May Sasaki
Shosuke Sasaki
Floyd Schmoe
Seattle Betsuin
Seattle Chinese Post
Seattle City Council
Seattle Post-Intelligencer
Seattle Public Library,
   Betty Tong-Lao
Seattle Times
Security Pacific Bank
Ben Segawa
Stan Shikuma
Bob Shimabukuro
Nobue Shimizu
Sakiko and Roger Shimizu
Dolores Sibonga
Rod Slemmons
Sam Solberg
Alan Sugiyama
Ed Suguro
Steve Sumida
Yoshi Suzuki
Olivia Taguinod
Calvin Takagi
Fred Takagi
Vicki Takamori

Henry Takayoshi
Yutaka "Dutch" Takekawa
Henry Taketa
Yasuko Takezawa
Keiko Taki
Gail Tanaka
Jere Thornton
Dr. Terrance Toda
Shokichi and Elsie Tokita
Tama Tokuda
Ryo Tsai
Yoshiko Tsujii
Michi Tsukada
Mayumi Tsutakawa
Tom Tsutakawa
Greg Tuai
Del Uchida
University of Washington
   Library, Karyl Winn
Shigeko Uno
Ken Wagner
Washington State Archives,
   Philippa Stairs
Barry Wong
Dean Wong
Paula Onodera Wong
Robert Yamada
Dorothy Yamaguchi
Frank Yamasaki
Fujie Yamasaki
Sadie Yamasaki
Sara Yamasaki
Margaret Yanagimachi
Henry Yorozu
May and Kaz Yoshinaka
Karen Yoshitomi

David A. Takami expanded the catalog he wrote for a 1992 Wing Luke Asian Museum exhibition on Japanese American history into this book. He is the author of *Shared Dreams: A History of Asians and Pacific Americans in Washington State* and numerous feature articles appearing in the *Washington Post, Seattle Times, Seattle Weekly, International Examiner,* and other publications.